Hazelden Co-occurring Disorders Program

Integrated Services for Substance Use and Mental Health Problems

D1232559

Screening and Assessment for People with Co-occurring Disorders

Mark McGovern, Ph.D.
and other faculty from the Geisel School of Medicine at Dartmouth

HAZELDEN®

Hazelden
Center City, Minnesota 55012
hazelden.org

ISBN: 978-1-59285-687-9

Editor's note

Alcoholics Anonymous, AA, and the Big Book are registered trademarks of Alcoholics Anonymous World Services, Inc.

The terms *mental health disorder, mental health problem,* and *psychiatric disorder* are all used interchangeably throughout the Co-occurring Disorders Program. These three terms refer to a non-severe diagnosis. The selection of terms used in each component of the program may reflect the preference of the individual author.

Cover design by Terri Kinne
Interior design by Kinne Design
Typesetting by Kinne Design and Madeline Berglund
Handout illustrations by David Swanson

▼

ABOUT THE AUTHORS

Mark McGovern

Mark McGovern, Ph.D., is a Professor of Psychiatry and of Community and Family Medicine at the Geisel School of Medicine at Dartmouth in Lebanon, New Hampshire. He practices at the Dartmouth Hitchcock Medical Center, and his research program is based at the Dartmouth Psychiatric Research Center. His clinical and research focus is integrated treatment for persons with co-occurring substance use and psychiatric disorders. Dr. McGovern has received a NIDA career development award and federal research grant funding to translate evidence-based therapies for co-occurring disorders into routine clinical settings. He has also received awards from the Robert Wood Johnson Foundation and the Substance Abuse and Mental Health Services Administration to advance a series of organizational measures of integrated service capacity. These measures, the Dual Diagnosis Capability in Addiction Treatment (DDCAT), Dual Diagnosis Capability in Mental Health Treatment (DDCMHT) and Dual Diagnosis Capability in Health Care Settings (DDCHCS), have been widely adopted and are being used to implement evidence-based treatments in community settings throughout the United States. Dr. McGovern has been actively involved in the education of medical students, psychiatric residents and fellows, and clinical psychology interns at Dartmouth and previously at Northwestern University Medical School in Chicago. Since 2009, he has been the editor-in-chief for the *Journal of Substance Abuse Treatment*, the leading scientific journal dedicated to addiction treatment research and implementation.

Robert E. Drake

Robert E. Drake, M.D., Ph.D., is the Andrew Thomson Professor of Psychiatry and of Community and Family Medicine at the Geisel School of Medicine at Dartmouth and the director of the Dartmouth Psychiatric Research Center. He has been at Dartmouth since 1984 and is currently vice chair and director of research in the Department of Psychiatry. He works as a community mental health doctor and researcher. His research focuses on co-occurring disorders, vocational rehabilitation, health services research, and evidence-based practices. He has written more than twenty books and more than 500 papers about co-occurring disorders, vocational rehabilitation, mental health services, evidence-based practices, and shared decision making.

Matthew R. Merrens

Matthew R. Merrens, Ph. D., has served as codirector of the Dartmouth Evidence-Based Practices Center and as visiting professor of psychiatry at Dartmouth Medical School. He received his Ph.D. in clinical psychology at the University of Montana and was

Duplicating this page is illegal. Do not copy this material without written permission from the publisher.

iii

formerly on the faculty and the chair of the Psychology Department at the State University of New York at Plattsburgh. He has extensive experience in clinical psychology and community mental health and has authored and edited textbooks on the psychology of personality, introductory psychology, the psychology of development, and social psychology. He recently published a book on evidence-based mental health practices and has also served as director of the Dartmouth Summer Institute in Evidence-Based Psychiatry and Mental Health.

Kim T. Mueser

Kim T. Mueser, Ph.D., is a clinical psychologist, executive director of the Center for Psychiatric Rehabilitation, and professor in the Departments of Occupational Therapy, Psychiatry, and Psychology at Boston University. Dr. Mueser's clinical and research interests include the treatment of co-occurring psychiatric and substance use disorders, family psychoeducation, psychiatric rehabilitation for serious mental illnesses, and the treatment of posttraumatic stress disorder. His research has been supported by the National Institute of Mental Health, the National Institute on Drug Abuse, the Substance Abuse and Mental Health Administration, and the National Alliance for Research on Schizophrenia and Depression. He is the co-author of more than ten books and treatment manuals and has published numerous articles in peer-reviewed journals. Dr. Mueser has also given numerous lectures and workshops on the treatment of co-occurring disorders and psychiatric rehabilitation, both nationally and internationally.

Mary F. Brunette

Mary F. Brunette, M.D., is an Associate Professor of Psychiatry at the Geisel School of Medicine at Dartmouth. She has been working in the field of treatment for patients with co-occurring disorders for twenty years. She conducts research on services and medications for people with co-occurring substance use and serious mental illness. She is a clinician who provides treatment for patients with co-occurring disorders. She also is medical director of the Bureau of Behavioral Health in the New Hampshire Department of Health and Human Services. She has published more than fifty articles and book chapters, many related to medication treatment for people with co-occurring disorders. She speaks nationally on this topic.

• • •

Hazelden Co-occurring Disorders Program

Integrated Services for Substance Use and Mental Health Problems

PROGRAM COMPONENTS

The Co-occurring Disorders Program is made up of a guidebook, five curricula, and a DVD. These components can stand alone, but when used together they provide a comprehensive, evidence-based program for the treatment of persons with co-occurring substance use and psychiatric disorders.

 ⬅ ***A Leader's Guide to Implementing Integrated Services***
Includes a guidebook and a CD-ROM.

Screening and Assessment ➡
Includes a clinician's guide and a CD-ROM.

 ⬅ ***Integrating Combined Therapies: Motivational Enhancement Therapy, Cognitive-Behavioral Therapy, and Twelve Step Facilitation***
Includes a clinician's guide and a CD-ROM.

Cognitive-Behavioral Therapy ➡
Includes a clinician's guide and a CD-ROM.

 ⬅ ***Medication Management***
Includes a clinician's guide and a CD-ROM.

Family Program: Education, Skills, and Therapy ➡
Includes a clinician's guide and a CD-ROM.

 ⬅ ***A Guide for Living with Co-occurring Disorders: Help and Hope for Clients and Their Families***
Ninety-minute DVD.

▼

CONTENTS

▼

ACKNOWLEDGMENTS

There is, in essence, nothing original in the *Screening and Assessment Clinician's Guide.* Collectively, our colleagues, over time and through today, have been striving diligently to improve the detection, identification, and nosological systems for persons with co-occurring psychiatric and substance use disorders. Efforts have been focused on precision, parsimony, and validity, with the intention of defining meaningful patient types and symptom clusters that may be associated with differential etiology, illness course, treatments, and outcomes.

We are especially indebted to the work of the American Psychiatric Association *(DSM-5),* the American Society of Addiction Medicine *(ASAM-PPC-3),* M. J. Alexander and colleagues (Modified Mini Screen), J. F. X. Carroll and J. J. McGinley (Mental Health Screening Form–III), L. S. Radloff (Center for Epidemiologic Studies Depression Scale), D. D. Blake and colleagues (Life Events Checklist), E. B. Blanchard and colleagues (PTSD Checklist), R. Mattick and C. Clarke (Social Interaction Anxiety Scale), and D. V. Sheehan and colleagues (Mini International Neuropsychiatric Interview). We have assembled the ingredients for this manual from the excellent work of these professionals and have either combined with others or adapted them here for their clinical appropriateness for persons with co-occurring disorders. Without the great work of these research scientists and instrument developers, this assembly would not have been possible. Our goal was to combine and adapt these measures in one single resource. Our hope was to develop a practical guide that would be useful to clinicians and helpful to patients.

In utilizing these measures for the purposes of treatment quality improvement, we are appreciative of the Network for the Improvement of Addiction Treatment (NIATx), most notably David Gustafson and Dennis McCarty. We are also indebted to the leadership, staff, and patients of Comprehensive Options for Drug Abuse (CODA, Inc.) in Portland, Oregon, the Hartford Dispensary in Hartford and New Britain, Connecticut, and the Addiction Treatment Program at Dartmouth-Hitchcock Medical Center in Hanover, New Hampshire, for field testing many of the measures in this manual.

Last but not least, we are grateful to Erica Ligeski, for her steady efforts to organize, simplify, and refine all the ingredients to this guide.

• • •

▼

INTRODUCTION

What Is This Guide About?

The order of components in the Co-occurring Disorders Program corresponds to the sequence of events in a clinician's relationship with a patient: (1) screening and assessment; (2) negotiating a treatment plan; (3) delivering and monitoring a treatment and assessing patient response; and (4) connecting the patient to supports—naturally occurring, professional, and peer support—that will augment the recovery process. Without the first step, it will be virtually impossible for a patient (or provider) to progress through the subsequent stages. Co-occurring disorders must be seen and identified. This guide, *Screening and Assessment for People with Co-occurring Disorders,* is intended to assist the frontline clinician in detecting, identifying, classifying, and monitoring changes in co-occurring substance use and psychiatric disorders. Being able to do this is the essential first step in the treatment process.

For the sake of convenience, the word "clinician" refers to any practitioner—counselors, supervisors, therapists, psychologists, facilitators, medical and mental health personnel, administrators, agency directors, and doctors—using these guides and curricula as part of the Co-occurring Disorders Program with patients and family members.

If My Primary Focus Is on Addictive Disorders, How Does This Guide Fit with My Work?

Historically, in addiction treatment settings, psychiatric "symptoms" were considered to be secondary to substance use. These symptoms were believed to be primarily associated with the effects of substances. From depression to anxiety to hallucinations, most symptoms were understood to be a result of intoxication, withdrawal, or cravings. Treatment, therefore, was directly focused on supporting patients through the period of intoxication and withdrawal by keeping them medically and socially safe. The initiation of abstinence officially started once the more acute symptoms of withdrawal had passed. During this phase, treatment planning and some actual treatment began. Psychiatric symptoms were still understood within the context of "Life on life's terms," and the patient's sometimes overwhelming experiences of emotion were seen as normal processes consistent with being newly sober.

Patients in traditional Twelve Step programs learned that some of these problems, particularly those that were long-standing, might be associated with character defects. These character defects would be the subject of analysis in Step Four of the Twelve Steps, and processing with a trusted other in Step Five. Continuing work on these defects would take place in Steps Six and Seven. Many of these issues were believed to be related to the core disease of alcoholism or addiction, and by working a solid and continuing program of recovery, the rough edges of these issues would be sanded down. Or at least they would become less central in the recovering patient's day-to-day life and relationships.

Indeed, many patients with co-occurring disorders probably benefit from and make great strides with this approach. Patients with mild depression, perhaps in the absence of the effects of alcohol, gain a more positive outlook and self-esteem, and become less isolating by using cognitive strategies (practicing acceptance, decreasing unrealistic self-blame and guilt) and positive coping skills (asking for help, spirituality). Patients with social phobia, perhaps in the absence of the effects of benzodiazepines, make dramatic gains in social avoidance and terror about public speaking, meeting new people, or being assertive by gradually developing trust, decreasing negative expectations, and becoming more comfortable in group situations. On the other hand, research has shown that not everyone benefits from traditional treatments. Many drop out early; many do not respond even after multiple treatment episodes or several cycles in and out of peer support groups. Some deteriorate and die, or become incarcerated or institutionalized (McLellan et al. 2000). Most commonly, patients with these disorders *never* even get treatment or exposure to peer support groups (Grant et al. 2004).

With this evidence in mind, it is now widely accepted that patients with co-occurring disorders may have a less-than-average chance of benefiting from traditional treatments. There is little evidence that addressing the substance use problem by itself will directly and positively affect the mental health problem, especially if the problem is of at least moderate severity and persistence and meets criteria for a psychiatric disorder.

Being able to accurately identify who has a co-occurring disorder, and the severity and type, is certainly the first step in understanding a patient at risk for being a nonresponder to treatment, and perhaps at risk for premature departure (i.e., dropout) and relapse. Once patients with these disorders have been identified, a treatment plan to address their problems can be developed, which will increase the chances for treatment completion, positive benefit, and a successful recovery.

If My Primary Focus Is on Psychiatric Disorders, How Does This Guide Fit with My Work?

For several reasons, most patient substance use problems are not detected in mental health settings. Professionals may not be adequately trained; patients themselves may believe that substance use is not the purview or business of mental health practitioners; and few practices may be in place to screen, assess, or diagnose substance-related conditions. Mental health providers have historically assumed that patients with alcohol or drug problems will seek treatment at specialized treatment programs, staffed by specialized treatment providers. In fact, most patients with substance use disorders will never seek or get treatment. Most of those who do will present in primary care and mental health settings rather than specialized addiction treatment programs. Mental health providers have been able to identify the more obvious cases of substance-related problems, such as when a patient presents for appointments in obvious intoxicated states. Detection is also possible when the patient chooses to reveal substance use as a chief complaint. In studies of detection of substance-related problems in mental health settings, the findings reveal that only 5 percent to 10 percent of persons with substance use problems, co-morbid with mental health problems, are correctly identified (Harris and Edlund 2005). Interestingly, substance-related disorders are much less likely to be detected or diagnosed to the degree to which patients are female, white, professional, and insured.

Patients in mental health settings with undiagnosed substance-related problems have been found to have less favorable outcomes than patients with mental health problems only (Drake, O'Neal, and Wallach 2008). Their psychiatric symptoms and substance use are not treated, and patients more often drop out of treatment or miss appointments. One study (Margules and Zweben 1998) even found that patients with substance use and co-occurring disorders on mental health providers' caseloads were more likely to be transferred to other practitioners within the clinic. In addition, therapists or doctors were more likely to cancel their appointments. Ironically, these results applied to cases with *undetected* substance use problems!

Even when substance-related problems were detected, many mental health providers conceptualized these problems as "symptoms" of underlying conditions. This treatment approach targeted the primary problem, such as depression, interpersonal problems, low self-esteem, or anxiety, and assumed substance use as a maladaptive coping or "self-medication" strategy. Even today, this approach to co-morbid disorders likely persists among mental health providers as the most common technique or model in routine practice settings. A recent review of medication studies of co-occurring depression and substance use disorders found that antidepressant medications had no effect on either substance use or depression if taken in isolation (i.e., without integrated or concurrent treatment focused on the substance use disorder) (Nunes and Levin 2004).

There is no evidence that addressing the mental health problem by itself will directly and positively affect the substance use problem, if the substance use problem is at the level of substance-related disorder.

Are the Primary Addiction and Primary Mental Health Approaches Still the Most Common?

As outlined in *A Leader's Guide to Implementing Integrated Services for People with Co-occurring Disorders,* researchers in mental health and addiction treatment services continue to find that the prevailing approach to psychiatric problems in addiction treatment settings is "addiction-only services," and the approach to substance-related problems in mental health settings is "mental-health-only services." Although the number of providers and practitioners offering dual diagnosis capable (DDC) or integrated services is growing, the majority (60 percent to 70 percent) of mental health and addiction providers still have primarily single disease approaches (McGovern, Matzkin, and Giard 2007).

By using the tools provided in this guide, practitioners will take the first step toward improving services for their patients with co-occurring disorders. This step, as with other steps in processes of change, may be the hardest one to initiate. But, once taken, this first step, screening and assessment, will turn out to be the most important and transformational in enhancing co-occurring treatment services.

How Can I Use This Guide Successfully?

Screening and Assessment is intended to be a practical clinical guide to screening and assessment of mental health problems in the context of substance use disorders. Since we will also address the presence of substance use problems co-existing with psychiatric disorders, the guide may also be useful in mental health settings.

This guide addresses the complexities involved in distinguishing between psychiatric disorders and substance-induced disorders. Clinical skill is necessary to apply this information to patient care. We advise clinical supervision, specifically by an appropriately trained, certified, licensed, and/or competent professional.

Screening measures for the most common psychiatric disorders are provided on the accompanying CD-ROM as PDFs that can be printed using a computer. These materials are ready for immediate implementation. (See pages 35–36 for sample thumbnail views of these measures.)

Following the discussion of screening measures, we describe the framework for a good clinical assessment for co-occurring disorders. Although standardized assessment tools exist, they are not included in this guide, as several of the best validated ones are proprietary. If the program or practitioner decides to utilize proprietary measures, information is included on how to order them. We do provide our own clinical assessment forms for various psychiatric disorders on the CD-ROM. (See page 48 for a sample thumbnail view.)

We present information about the *Diagnostic and Statistical Manual of Mental Disorders, Fifth Edition (DSM-5)* differential diagnoses of substance-induced versus independent psychiatric disorders. This review should also help the clinician distinguish between substance use and psychiatric disorders and begin to plan treatment accordingly.

Treatment planning, especially planning that incorporates patient motivation and treatment preferences, is a key theme of this guide. An index for assessing a patient's motivation to address co-occurring problems and treatments, the Stage of Motivation and Treatment Readiness for Co-occurring Disorders (SOMTR-COD), is included on the CD-ROM. (See page 56 for a thumbnail view.) It can be immediately implemented in practice settings. This form will help guide conversations with patients on how they want to focus their change efforts. Obviously, the clinician may have other ideas about these efforts and choose to negotiate treatment, suggest more careful monitoring, and begin to deliver motivational enhancement therapy for co-occurring disorders (see *Integrating Combined Therapies for People with Co-occurring Disorders*).

After a treatment plan has been negotiated, the clinician can record it on the Comprehensive Recovery Plan template, included on the CD-ROM. (See page 63 for a thumbnail view.) This form can be used as a document of understanding between the patient and the clinician regarding the path for working together to achieve treatment goals.

In aggregate, quality assurance or process improvements at the program or clinic level can address recurrent treatment problems. Concrete suggestions on how to collect and study these data are also provided.

We hope these materials help you to more accurately and reliably identify the types of problems from which your patients suffer. Identifying and discussing these issues with your patients is likely to improve their chances for successful recovery and eventually improve outcomes.

•   •   •

Prevalence of Psychiatric Disorders in Addiction Treatment

KEY QUESTIONS RAISED IN CHAPTER 1:

1. How common are co-occurring disorders?

2. What disorders should I expect in clinical practice?

The Rationale for Considering Prevalence

Prudence suggests that people should plan for high-probability events. An 80 percent chance of rain may warrant grabbing an umbrella upon leaving for work. On the other hand, when you buy a ticket for a $20 million lottery, you usually do not make preparations for winning because there is such a remote chance that will happen.

A higher prevalence or occurrence of certain psychiatric problems in addiction treatment settings may suggest that clinicians develop a plan for response. Higher rates of one disorder versus another may help you to decide the kind of treatments you want to offer, the materials you want to obtain for patient and family education, or even the way you want to organize relationships with other treatment providers. Prevalence rates should certainly suggest the likelihood of the presentation of disorders, and perhaps the thoroughness with which you might try to identify and/or assess these problems.

In contrast, disorders that are less common or even rare in the population may not require as much attention in your treatments, community provider relationships, or screening and assessment.

Deciding what disorders to focus on can be determined by the rates these disorders occur at your center or clinic.

Population-based Studies

Epidemiological, or population-based, studies are normally based on interviews. Essentially, a representative sample is selected, and trained personnel conduct structured diagnostic interviews in community settings. Persons must agree to these interviews, and they are compensated for their participation.

Regier and colleagues published the best-known study addressing the issue of co-occurring disorders in 1990 (see figure 1 on the next page). Among a sample of close to 10,000 adults across the United States, of those with alcohol use disorders, about one-third (36 percent) had a psychiatric disorder. And of those with a drug use disorder, over half (53.1 percent) had a psychiatric disorder. The odds of having a psychiatric disorder, if the person had an alcohol use disorder or drug use disorder, escalated two- and fourfold, respectively. In other words, if you have a patient with an alcohol use disorder, it is a good bet that the patient will also have a psychiatric disorder; and if you have a patient with a drug use disorder, there is an even greater chance.

FIGURE 1

Co-morbidity of Substance Use and Psychiatric Disorders

Among a sample of about 10,000 adults:

- 13.5% had an alcohol use disorder. Of those, 36.6% also had a psychiatric disorder.

- 6.1% had a drug use disorder. Of those, 53.1% also had a psychiatric disorder.

- 22.5% had a psychiatric disorder. Of those, 28.9% also had an alcohol or drug use disorder.

	%	ODDS RATIO
Alcohol Use	13.5	
Psychiatric Disorder	36.6	2.3
Drug Use	6.1	
Psychiatric Disorder	53.1	4.5
Psychiatric Disorder	22.5	
Alcohol or Drug Disorder	28.9	2.7

Source: Regier et al. 1990

These investigators also examined the rates of substance use disorders among those with specific psychiatric disorders. Of those with a psychiatric disorder, 25 percent to 33 percent also had a substance use disorder (alcohol or drug). Figure 2 displays the lifetime rates of these co-occurring disorders. The table shows that for patients with bipolar disorders and schizophrenia, substance use disorders are of considerable prevalence. Patients with other mood disorders (such as depression) and anxiety disorders are also at great risk.

Several population-based studies have focused on the prevalence of co-occurring substance use disorders, and there is remarkable convergence in findings, even though the methods for these studies varied (Clark et al. 2008).

FIGURE 2

Lifetime Prevalence of Substance Use Disorders for Psychiatric Disorders

PSYCHIATRIC DISORDER	% ANY SUBSTANCE ABUSE/ DEPENDENCE
General Population	16.7
Schizophrenia	47.0
Any Affective Disorder	32.0
Any Bipolar Disorder	56.1
Major Depression	27.2
Persistent Depressive Disorder	31.4
Any Anxiety Disorder	23.7
Obsessive Compulsive Disorder	32.8

Source: Regier et al. 1990

One of the more recent studies (Grant et al. 2004) had substantially improved methods, and, in particular, was careful to distinguish between substance-induced disorders and independent psychiatric disorders. This study also focused on the most common disorders in the population: mood, substance use, and anxiety disorders. These disorders, taken together, probably affect as many as sixty million persons in the United States alone.

FIGURE 3

Twelve-Month Prevalence of Index Substance Use and Co-occurring Mood and Anxiety Disorders

INDEX DIAGNOSIS	% CO-MORBID MOOD	% CO-MORBID ANXIETY	% CO-MORBID SUBSTANCE USE
Any Substance Use Disorder	19.67	17.71	
Alcohol	18.85	17.05	
Drug	31.80	25.36	
Mood Disorder			19.97
Anxiety Disorder			14.96

Source: Grant et al. 2004

As figure 3 shows, the overlap in disorders is consistent with the studies by Regier and colleagues. About one in five persons with a substance use disorder had either an anxiety disorder or a mood disorder. Persons with drug use disorders were more likely than those with alcohol use disorders to have a psychiatric problem. Persons with mood disorders were slightly more likely than those with anxiety disorders to have a co-occurring substance use disorder.

Prevalence of Psychiatric Disorders among Patients in Treatment

Much like any medical condition, there is probably a difference between people who have a problem and do not seek treatment and those who do seek treatment. Among other factors, one may assume that those who seek treatment are suffering greater degrees of severity or impairment. Of course, it may also be the case that any individual with a disease may not seek care because of geographic, financial, cultural, informational, or other matters of access.

Nevertheless, when the Grant study examined the rates of co-occurring disorders among those seeking treatment (versus those who did not), the degree of overlap skyrocketed, particularly among those with substance use disorders (see figure 4). This does suggest that among patients seeking treatment, co-occurring disorders are found two or three times the rate expected in the general population.

FIGURE 4

Twelve-Month Prevalence of Index Substance Use and Co-occurring Mood and Anxiety Disorders of Treated Persons

INDEX DIAGNOSIS	% CO-MORBID MOOD	% CO-MORBID ANXIETY	% CO-MORBID SUBSTANCE USE
Any Substance Use Disorder	NA	NA	
Alcohol	40.69	33.98	
Drug	60.31	42.63	
Mood Disorder			20.78
Anxiety Disorder			16.51

Source: Grant et al. 2004

In 2001, Cacciola and colleagues from the University of Pennsylvania reviewed the literature on prevalence rates of psychiatric disorders in addiction treatment settings. To date, this has been the best and most comprehensive review of prevalence rates in addiction treatment settings. Similarly, the most thorough single study has been by Ross, Glaser, and Germanson (1988). (See figure 5.)

FIGURE 5

Psychiatric Disorders in Addiction Treatment

Two studies of prevalence rates in addiction treatment settings had similar findings. Persons with substance use disorders are also likely to have mood and anxiety disorders.

DISORDER	CACCIOLA	ROSS
Mood Disorder	10–45%	31.4%
Anxiety Disorder	10–46%	45.4%
Post-traumatic Stress Disorder	15–45%	NA
Antisocial Personality Disorder	25–50%	36.5%
Borderline Personality Disorder	10–30%	NA
Schizophrenia	< 5%	4.3%

Source: Cacciola et al. 2001; Ross, Glaser, and Germanson 1988

The Cacciola review notes the wide "bands" of variability in prevalence rates across a number of studies. The variability found by Cacciola is initially quite striking and results from the different measures, methods, settings, populations, and diagnostic criteria used across studies. Nonetheless, a consistent pattern begins to emerge. Much like with the population-based studies, persons with substance use disorders, and even more so among those seeking treatment, are likely to suffer from mood and anxiety disorders.

Cacciola also observed relatively high, though perhaps less than expected, rates of personality disorders. Next to mood and anxiety disorders, patients with antisocial personality disorders compose the largest group of patients with psychiatric disorders in addiction treatment. Some researchers have argued that personality disorders, in particular antisocial personality disorder, cannot be reliably diagnosed because of the considerable overlap with drug use behaviors. These behaviors may include larceny, robbery, and burglary to obtain money for drugs, disregard of laws to support drug use, and violation of social norms and relationship commitments as a consequence of addiction.

A more recent study (McGovern et al. 2006, which is included on the CD-ROM) surveyed frontline addiction treatment providers as to the prevalence of specific psychiatric disorders in program settings. Over 450 providers were surveyed, and remarkably, the estimates were consistent with the research studies. As figure 6 shows, mood disorders (including dysthymia and major depression), anxiety disorders (including generalized anxiety disorder, panic disorder, social phobia,

FIGURE 6

Addiction Treatment Provider Estimates by Psychiatric Disorder

Mood disorders, anxiety disorders, and post-traumatic stress disorder were cited most often among patients seeking treatment.

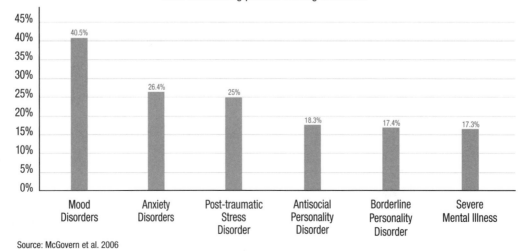

Source: McGovern et al. 2006

Clinical Disorders

These include various disorders and conditions related to symptoms and impairments in functioning. Diagnosis is typically related to the current presentation, but can also be reviewed for its presence over a person's lifetime. The table below lists the primary clinical disorders according to *DSM-5*.

- Disorders usually first diagnosed in infancy, childhood, or adolescence (excluding intellectual disabilities)
- Delirium, dementia, and amnestic and other cognitive disorders
- Mental disorders due to a general medical condition
- Substance-related disorders
- Schizophrenia and other psychotic disorders
- Mood disorders
- Anxiety disorders
- Somatoform disorders
- Factitious disorders
- Dissociative disorders
- Sexual and gender identity disorders
- Eating disorders
- Sleep disorders
- Impulse-control disorders not elsewhere classified
- Adjustment disorders
- Other conditions that may be a focus of clinical attention

Personality Disorders

These include various personality disorders related to long-standing maladaptive functioning, particularly in relation to self and others. They can usually be traced to childhood or adolescence and are constellations of maladaptive behaviors, interpersonal relationships, and self-regulatory patterns. The table below lists the primary personality disorders according to *DSM-5*.

- Paranoid personality disorder
- Schizoid personality disorder
- Schizotypal personality disorder
- Antisocial personality disorder
- Borderline personality disorder
- Histrionic personality disorder
- Narcissistic personality disorder
- Avoidant personality disorder
- Dependent personality disorder
- Obsessive-compulsive personality disorder
- Personality disorder not otherwise specified
- Intellectual disabilities

Duplicating this page is illegal. Do not copy this material without written permission from the publisher.

13

and obsessive compulsive disorder), and post-traumatic stress disorder (PTSD) were cited the most often as co-morbidities among patients presenting for services. Borderline personality (BP) and antisocial personality (AP) disorders were also common, and patients with severe mental illnesses (such as schizophrenia, bipolar disorder, or schizoaffective disorder) were rare. Patients with bipolar disorder accounted for most of the estimates in the severe mental illness (SMI) category.

Barlow (2002) reviewed the relative chronology of onset of mental health and substance use disorders and found that among anxiety disorders, both generalized anxiety and panic disorders are more likely to occur during or develop secondarily to substance use. In contrast, two other anxiety disorders, PTSD and social phobia, have been found by researchers to predate the onset of the substance use disorder. As such, PTSD and social phobia are most likely to be independent psychiatric disorders. Longitudinal studies (those following a large group of people over an extended period of time) are still needed to tease out the patterns of order of other co-occurring disorders.

Several disorders have been reported to be common but have been less carefully researched for prevalence as co-occurring disorders. Among these are attention deficit and hyperactivity disorder, personality disorders other than antisocial or borderline, sleep disorders, and sexual dysfunctions and gender dysphoria. Therefore, these disorders are currently less understood from an evidence-based perspective (SAMHSA 2002; McGovern and McLellan 2008).

Based on the review of prevalence in the general population and clinical settings, prudence suggests that patients with substance use disorders, and those who care for them, may need a plan for the following disorders, in order of relative likelihood:

1. Mood disorders (including persistent depressive disorder and major depression)

2. Anxiety disorders (including generalized anxiety, panic disorder, agoraphobia, and specific phobias)

3. Obsessive-compulsive and related disorders

4. Post-traumatic stress disorder

5. Social anxiety disorder (its likely independence from substance use disorder may also warrant special consideration, as should the fact that persons with social anxiety may avoid treatment because of primarily group formats)

6. Bipolar disorder

Patients with substance use disorders need to learn about these disorders, and practitioners need to be able to accurately detect and potentially treat them. Given their common overlap with substance use disorders, neglecting these disorders in practice will likely result in less favorable outcomes.

Although prevalent, personality disorders may require even more developed assessment protocols and more time for observation and assessment for accurate diagnostics. This is especially true for those with co-occurring disorders. Refer to Crouse, Drake, and McGovern (2007) for information on the prevalence, assessment, and treatment for co-occurring personality and substance use disorders. ▼

KEY POINTS ADDRESSED IN CHAPTER

1

1. Psychiatric disorders co-exist in 20 percent to 30 percent of persons with substance use disorders, and these rates double (40 percent to 60 percent) in treatment settings.

2. Substance use disorders co-exist in 20 percent to 50 percent of persons with psychiatric disorders, and these rates also increase, depending on the disorder, in treatment settings.

3. Depression, anxiety, PTSD, social anxiety disorder, and bipolar disorder are the most common co-occurring conditions among patients with substance use disorders in addiction treatment.

4. Either alcohol or drug problems are common among patients with psychiatric disorders.

Complexities of Assessment

Five key factors often add to the complexity of assessing for psychiatric disorders among patients who also have substance use disorders:

1. Intoxication
2. Withdrawal
3. Substance-induced disorders
4. Motivational factors
5. Understanding the differences among feelings, symptoms, and disorders

Intoxication

Persons under the influence of drugs and alcohol are in altered mental and emotional states. This is the primary reason people initially use addictive substances: to change how they feel. Interestingly, this is often the reason people cite as to why they relapsed to substances even when in recovery: to change how they feel.

Figure 7, shown on page 18, describes the most common negative affects or emotions associated with specific substances. Note how easy it would be to confuse these "states" with symptoms associated with psychiatric disorders. In other words, these states could *mimic* psychiatric disorders.

A person who uses alcohol may seek to feel less inhibited, to become more social, or to anesthetize underlying bad feelings. Continued use of alcohol, however, will eventually yield the emotional state of depression.

Similarly, benzodiazepines, such as Klonopin or Xanax, will be sought to relieve anxiety, but over time they become associated with more depressed emotional states.

Cocaine and other stimulants produce a positive and grandiose sense of self, expansiveness, and euphoria, and these affective states can persist but are also accompanied by anxiety, depression, and rapid shifts in mood.

FIGURE 7

Substances and Negative Emotions

SUBSTANCE	NEGATIVE EMOTIONAL STATE	MIMICKED PSYCHIATRIC DISORDER
Alcohol	Depression; Anxiety	Mood Disorder; Anxiety Disorder
Benzodiazepines	Depression; Anxiety	Mood Disorder; Anxiety Disorder
Cocaine/Amphetamine/ Methamphetamine	Depression; Anxiety; Mood Swings; Impulsivity	Anxiety Disorder; Bipolar Disorder
Cannabis/Marijuana	Depression; Anxiety	Mood Disorder; Anxiety Disorder
Opiates/Heroin/ Prescription Narcotics	Depression	Mood Disorder
Polysubstance (Mixed Substance Use)	Depression; Anxiety; Mood Swings; Impulsivity	Mood Disorder; Anxiety Disorder; Bipolar Disorder

Cannabis has complex emotional effects. It is similar to alcohol and cocaine, and to some hallucinogenic substances as well. Persons who are high from marijuana may feel detached, internally preoccupied, or euphoric. These states may be accompanied by depressed, acutely self-conscious, or anxious moods.

Opioids, including heroin and prescription narcotics such as hydrocodone (Vicodin) and oxycodone (OxyContin), are analgesics and have a numbing and reality-distancing effect. Patients under the influence of these substances may seem euphoric or detached, but may also mimic symptoms of depression while intoxicated.

Up to half of patients presenting for addiction treatment may use more than one substance, and this adds to the challenge of determining the symptoms of intoxication as well as the mimicking of a psychiatric disorder. There are four methods to accurately determine what substance a patient used to become intoxicated:

1. Patient self-report

2. Collateral or informant report: family members, bystanders, associates

3. Observational information: witnessing use or traces of substances or paraphernalia

4. Toxicological data: urinalysis or Breathalyzer results

Evaluate carefully for the possibility of intoxication. The more methods or indicators used in the assessment, the more reliable the "rule-out" of the influence of the immediate physiological and psychological effects of substances.

Withdrawal

When the immediate effects of intoxication have worn off and the substances are evacuating the body, withdrawal sets in. Typically, this involves a homeostatic process where a patient's physiological processes rebound to a baseline state. During withdrawal, the symptoms and emotions are often the opposite of the desired effects of the substance. For patients who are substance dependent, rapid cycling of intoxication and withdrawal is typical. For patients meeting substance abuse criteria, more time may pass between periods of substance use and intoxication, so acute withdrawal may be easier to discern. There is no clear scientific information about the true duration of withdrawal, either from a physiological or psychological perspective. Physiological withdrawal is understood to happen more quickly and pass sooner than psychological withdrawal. For the purposes of assessing for psychiatric disorders, realistically, only physiological aspects of withdrawal can be considered.

The Clinical Institute for Withdrawal Assessment Scale lists thirteen common symptoms of withdrawal and asks the assessor to rate the presence and severity of withdrawal based on these items (see figure 8). Two of these items pertain directly to the most common psychiatric disorders (mood and anxiety). Many of the other items might be considered associated symptoms of mood disorders (memory problems, sleep disturbance, fatigue), anxiety disorders (irritability, sweating), or other disorders, including thought disorders.

FIGURE 8

Clinical Institute for Withdrawal Assessment Scale (CIWA)

COMMON SIGNS AND SYMPTOMS OF WITHDRAWAL		
• Anxiety	• Memory Problems	• Tremor
• Depressed Mood	• Psychosis	• Violence
• Hallucinations	• Sleep Disturbance	• Fatigue
• Irritability	• Tachycardia	• Anorexia
	• Sweating	

Source: *American Society of Addiction Medicine Patient Placement Criteria,*
3rd edition (ASAM PPC-3) 2013

Assessment for psychiatric disorders, therefore, must include a "rule-out" on the presence or absence of physiological withdrawal symptoms. For alcohol, symptoms may be present over forty-eight hours, for opiates over four weeks, and for other substances two weeks. These are rough guidelines and depend on the actual biomedical condition, metabolism, and other physiological factors, as well as the amount and duration of use for each patient.

Substance-Induced Disorders

The *DSM-5* distinguishes between substance-induced disorders and independent disorders. Several of the most common co-occurring psychiatric disorders—mood and anxiety disorders—are included in the list of potential substance-induced disorders.

This system for differential diagnostics will be described in detail in chapter 5. In general, for a psychiatric disorder to be deemed an independent disorder, it must be ascertained either to have been present before the onset of the substance use disorder (in chronological sequence) or to be present after a period of thirty days of abstinence or postwithdrawal at some point in the person's life or at present. In some instances this differential can be easily established, such as with PTSD or social anxiety disorders. But in other instances, including where substance use is ongoing without any period of abstinence, the differential may be challenging.

Motivational Factors

Many patients enter treatment for substance use disorders as a result of mandates from the criminal justice system, through probation and parole, DUI or drug court programs, or alternative sentencing. Other patients may enter treatment as a requirement of their employer or to maintain a professional license or certification. For these individuals, the initial goal in presenting for treatment is to minimize the number of problems, psychiatric or otherwise, and to fast-forward as rapidly as possible through their mandated requirements. This minimization pertains to substance use *and* psychiatric issues.

Other patients presenting for services may learn that their psychiatric problems exclude them from a program. So, for instance, it may be well-known among alcohol-dependent homeless men that a certain detoxification program does not admit patients with "psych" histories. When seeking shelter, these men know not to report psychiatric symptoms in order to gain admission.

In contrast, in other settings, the degree of severity, psychiatric or otherwise, may be to a patient's advantage in terms of the admission queue for a residential rehab or to get more medication (for instance, in a methadone maintenance program).

Lastly, the potential exists for a lack of trust in the early stage of treatment, especially during the admission process. A patient may realize that he or she has depression, PTSD, or social anxiety disorder but may doubt whether the practitioner can be trusted with this information, or may have reservations about the program's capacity to deal with these issues. In the case of both social phobia and PTSD, avoidance symptoms are diagnostic, so the patient may be disinclined to even want to think about, let alone talk about, these issues. Over time, however, as a patient becomes increasingly comfortable and trusting, it is quite possible that these symptoms will apparently surface or even seem to worsen. Instead of these being "new" symptoms or clinical deterioration, this report may actually be an indicator of patient (and clinician) progress.

Attention to "demand" characteristics, stigma and discrimination, and payoffs and motivational factors in reporting or not reporting psychiatric symptoms in addiction settings are critical. Likewise, in mental health settings, patients actively using substances, in particular illicit substances (cocaine, heroin, marijuana), may be equally subject to stigma, discrimination, and exclusion. Clinicians and programs collude with this pattern unless these issues are directly raised and assessed like any other mental health condition.

Feelings, Symptoms, Disorders

Every patient has feelings, many have symptoms, and some have disorders. Learning to differentiate among these is essential in the assessment process. For the patient, learning the difference is essential to the treatment and recovery process.

Traditional psychoanalytic approaches to addiction often viewed the patient's difficulty in managing painful emotions as the key to the treatment approach. These approaches never fully appreciated either the physical or social aspects to addictive disease, but they did underscore the role of emotion in the process of addiction and recovery. Slogans like "Life on life's terms," "Get real, feel, and deal," and "Stark raving sobriety" captured the new or recovering experience of an intense emotional life.

Edward Khantzian, one of the first and foremost addiction psychiatrists, once said that "alcoholics either feel too much or nothing at all." A person in early recovery experiences emotions that are, perhaps for the first time since childhood, unadulterated by substances. Some of these re-emerging feelings are experienced as positive; others are very uncomfortable, such as sadness and loss, fear and anxiety, guilt and shame, or anger.

Many patients will fear these feelings, and with growing discomfort seek immediate relief. In some cases, without new coping skills, this may lead to relapse. In other cases, this may involve trying to self-diagnose and seek a prescribed "medication" that will make the feelings stop.

Having these feelings, learning to label them, and managing them are principal challenges in the early recovery process, and perhaps for life. Many addiction treatment providers hang a poster in the treatment setting that illustrates emotions and facial expressions. A mood poster or handout can help facilitate the clinical interaction and the development of affect management skills. A handout illustrating different moods and emotions is provided on the CD-ROM for your use.

Feelings are normal affective responses to life. A full range can be expected. Symptoms including depression, anxiety, guilt, shame, irritability, sadness, distractibility, and sleeplessness may all occur, particularly after a change in substance use. As mentioned previously, these symptoms are often associated with withdrawal, intoxication, and the newfound experience of life without chemicals. Symptoms will likely occur in response to stimuli and will pass. Symptoms may also be isolated and not cluster into a series of criteria, as outlined in the *DSM-5*, to constitute a diagnosis.

If a person does have *DSM-5* symptoms and they are of sufficient duration, causing significant functional impairment, then he or she may meet criteria for a disorder. Feelings and symptoms pass in minutes, hours, or days. Disorders persist for weeks, months, or even years.

Feelings will need to be processed, symptoms will need to be managed, and disorders will need to be treated. ▼

KEY POINTS ADDRESSED IN CHAPTER

2

1. Several important factors must be considered when assessing for psychiatric problems among patients with substance-related disorders:

   - Is the patient intoxicated?

   - Is the patient experiencing withdrawal symptoms?

   - Is this a substance-induced or independent psychiatric disorder?

   - What is the patient's motivation to report or minimize psychiatric concerns?

2. Patients and providers can confuse "feelings," "symptoms," and "disorders." Feelings will need to be processed, symptoms will need to be managed, and disorders will need to be treated.

Duplicating this page is illegal. Do not copy this material without written permission from the publisher.

23

The Initial Clinical Process

KEY QUESTIONS RAISED IN CHAPTER 3:

1. What is screening?

2. What are the advantages of systematic screening for psychiatric problems?

3. What are the benefits to patients of systematic screening for psychiatric problems?

The Co-occurring Disorders Program addresses each stage of the therapeutic relationship between a practitioner or a program and the patient: access, engagement, and retention. *Access* essentially involves getting the patient into an initial assessment. *Engagement* entails connecting with the patient and establishing a treatment alliance, a therapeutic bond, and some agreement on the tactics, purposes, and goals of the relationship. *Retention* is the process wherein a treatment provider maintains the relationship with the patient over the course of the treatment episode, generally over a sufficient enough time so that the patient gets a therapeutic "dose," which will increase the chances of success.

This guide, *Screening and Assessment,* targets the initial stage of the encounter. During this stage, it is critically important to promote access for patients into treatment. Although aspects of retention are not the focus of this guide, they are key indicators of the quality of the initial clinical process. Chapter 10 will present more information about quality improvement approaches. You may also wish to refer to the work of the Network for the Improvement of Addiction Treatment (NIATx). See www.niatx.net for more information.

The relationship between patient and the practitioner or program is key to the effectiveness of this initial clinical process. This relationship can be described alternatively as the therapeutic alliance, nonspecific therapy factors, the therapeutic bond, or the working alliance. Common sense and evidence say that the relationship is the vehicle within which the technical aspects of assessment and treatment take place. A full description of the nature and dynamics of this relationship, however, is beyond the scope of this guide.

In considering the more technical aspects of the initial clinical process, we have organized the following chapters according to five key strategies:

1. Screening (chapters 3 and 4)

2. Assessment and differential diagnosis (chapters 5 and 6)

3. Treatment planning (chapter 7)

4. Shared decision making (chapter 8)

5. Treatment monitoring (chapters 9 and 10)

What Is Screening?

Screening is a rapid and brief test of the likely presence or absence of a symptom, problem, or disorder. Screening is the first step in the process of discerning whether a problem is likely. Screening is best if systematic. In other words, the same screening process should occur from patient to patient and from clinician to clinician. This ensures consistency in clinical practice and likely results in more predictable care for patients and families.

An example of a screening test outside of the addiction or mental health fields is the at-home pregnancy test. These tests can be purchased over the counter, and they are brief and relatively easy to administer. They yield information that suggests the presence or absence of pregnancy. If used as instructed, the tests are reliable and valid. The findings from the at-home pregnancy test are positively associated, at about 90 percent, with clinical examination.

In summary, screening

- detects the likely presence of a disorder

- is not a conclusive diagnosis

- is the first step in a process of discernment, clinical investigation, and examination

In routine settings, screening is often not used in a systematic manner. Sometimes, screening consists of only one or two questions. For example, to screen for depression, a practitioner may ask a patient these two questions: "Have you ever been diagnosed with depression?" and "Have you ever been prescribed medication for depression?" The answers to these questions, if negative, may permit the clinician to move on. Some practitioners mistakenly define the term "screening" quite literally, as "to screen something out." So, in some programs, an affirmative answer to these two questions may mean the person does not gain entry to the residential detoxification center.

Other approaches to screening rely solely on the art of the clinician. This practice typically entrusts the clinician to conduct a thorough, if somewhat idiosyncratic, interview to ascertain the likely presence or absence of a range of disorders. In some cases, the clinician is licensed or certified in his or her scope of practice to conduct these screenings; in other instances, staff members of varying expertise are involved in the initial process.

We recommend a more consistent and systematic approach to screening. Systematic and consistent approaches have many advantages over more idiosyncratic and clinician-driven approaches.

What Are the Advantages and Benefits of Brief, Systematic Screening?

Systematic screening is underutilized perhaps because providers lack information about screening measures, but also because they have been inclined to trust more artistic and idiosyncratic approaches to clinical practice. Because of this historical tendency, clinicians may have not been providing consistent assessments and, consequently, consistent treatments.

Here's a recent example: Jane, a counselor, attended a conference on trauma and PTSD over the weekend. She came to work on Monday with two assessments on her schedule. With the conference fresh in her mind, she was diligent to inquire and probe for trauma and PTSD symptoms. Both patients were found to have PTSD.

George, also a counselor at the clinic, spent the weekend with his daughter's dance troupe. He also had two assessments scheduled for Monday. George did not inquire about trauma or PTSD, so neither patient was found to have those issues.

Perhaps this inconsistency could have been circumvented if both Jane and George attended the same conference. But this is impractical. Also, given that workforce turnover is common in mental health and addiction treatment settings, what happens when one or both clinicians leave the clinic to take jobs in other programs?

In other words, systematic screening has benefits, both for consistency across clinicians and across patients presenting for services, and it also can be a technique to standardize in a practice setting.

Screening must be seen as a "first take" with a person, particularly one with a substance use disorder. If a screen turns out to be negative, perhaps it needs to be repeated at a later date or time. If it turns out to be positive, it may also need to be repeated at a later date and time. Much like the pregnancy test that gets repeated to verify the finding, a screening measure might be repeated to validate the initial score.

A frequently raised concern about more formal screening measures is the historical lack of trust in patient self-report. With respect to substance use behavior, there is an established tradition of "trust but verify" reported drug and alcohol use. Considering the factors outlined in chapter 2 (intoxication, withdrawal, substance-induced disorders, motivation), we believe the use of screening measures to obtain a rapid and brief survey of a patient's symptoms is good clinical practice.

Researchers who have studied the modality of self-report assessments have found that persons queried about sexual risk behavior and drug use were more likely to divulge highly confidential information about themselves to (1) a computer, (2) a paper-and-pencil survey, and (3) a trained clinical interviewer, in that order. In short, people are willing to reveal these kinds of symptoms when asked and, in many cases, feel both relieved and cared for when this happens (Chinman et al. 2002; Siegel, Krauss, and Karus 1994; Locke et al. 1992; Waterton and Duffy 1984; Turner et al. 1998; Erdman, Klein, and Greist 1985).

As discussed in chapter 2, screening for psychiatric issues in addiction settings among patients with substance use problems is complicated. For this reason, self-report screening measures, however economical, will need to be interpreted by a clinician. Neither assessment nor treatment decisions can be based on self-report information alone. Some programs that use standardized screening measures (to be discussed in chapter 4) have had to increase cutoffs since most patients score high when entering their services. These programs found that more reliable and accurate scores were higher than the recommended cutoffs.

Figure 9 summarizes the advantages and benefits of screening patients. For the practitioner and program, having a standardized and consistent screening process provides a common language among staff members within the program, and it can improve communication with providers outside the program or office. It provides a credible and objective measure beyond clinical impression and artful anecdote. Staff members use the same measure so clinician variability is reduced. Having screening measures on the front end of the treatment experience can help train new staff in intake and admission procedures. The same measure can be used as an individual patient treatment response or an indicator of program outcome

FIGURE 9

Advantages and Benefits of Screening

VALUE OF SCREENING MEASURES FOR CLINICIANS	VALUE OF SCREENING MEASURES FOR PATIENTS
• Systemizes intake and admission process • Provides a common language and an objective metric • Provides staff with a valid instrument • Facilitates training • Measures process and outcome	• A disorder, if present, may only be found if looked for. • A disorder, if present, may affect treatment participation. • A disorder, if present, may affect treatment outcomes. • A disorder, if present, may require specialized treatments.

quality. Using a screening measure for program evaluation will be described in chapter 10.

For patients, being screened in a systematic way is also a positive experience. Many providers have anxiety about asking a patient "personal" questions about psychological matters, as if inquiry about drug and alcohol use is any less invasive. Some providers have even speculated that asking these questions will "trigger" symptoms that the patient might not otherwise have. Other providers worry that by being asked psychiatric-symptom questions, patients with substance use disorders, much like hypochondriacal medical students learning about physical diseases, will develop concerns and self-diagnoses about all the symptoms assessed.

There is no scientific foundation to these concerns. In fact, the results are to the contrary. To the extent that patients are systematically asked questions about their psychological status, they typically feel they are taken seriously and responded to, and they consider the treatment provider in a more professional manner.

And perhaps most important, if a problem is identified, it can be assessed and diagnosed, which becomes the first step in a thorough treatment of a co-occurring psychiatric disorder. This will only serve to produce a better treatment outcome and an improved chance at recovery. ▼

1. Screening is a rapid and brief test for the presence or absence of a symptom or disorder.

2. Having a systematic screening measure provides a practitioner or program with a consistent approach to detecting co-occurring psychiatric problems, even in the presence of substance use disorders.

3. Patients do not have a negative reaction to screening measures and, in fact, experience them as positive, caring, and helpful in the path to recovery.

The Screening Process

Selecting a Screening Measure

A busy practitioner does not have the time to sort through the seemingly infinite number of screening measures that are available. Likewise, most program administrators lack the time or interest in locating a measure, and even more so, need to be careful about the costs involved in using screening measures. Although screening measures have been developed and are readily available, most practitioners and programs do not use them. As noted in chapter 3, practices for patients with co-occurring disorders can be improved with more systematic and consistent tools to *detect* psychiatric symptoms.

The purpose of this chapter is to help the practitioner or program leader select screening measures. We will address the things to consider when selecting these measures, the pros and cons of several measures, and how to use the measures we recommend. Selecting these measures is an individual choice, so we advise you to determine the best fit for your practice setting.

We provide you with both generic and specific screening measures for immediate implementation. They can be found on the accompanying CD-ROM. Thumbnail views appear where they are discussed in detail in this guide.

There are several important considerations in choosing a screening measure:

- relevance
- psychometric properties
- complexity
- cost

Relevance

First, relevance must be considered. It is important to select a measure that has some bearing on the issue, either during the assessment process or during

Duplicating this page is illegal. Do not copy this material without written permission from the publisher.

31

treatment. Choosing a measure that impacts neither of these would be less than wise. One criterion for relevance may be prevalence. Are you screening for something that is prevalent? From our review of prevalence rates in chapter 1, it would seem that a screening measure should assess, at the very least, for the presence of the most common disorders: mood disorders, anxiety disorders, PTSD, and social anxiety disorder. The measure may also screen for less common disorders, such as bipolar disorder, schizophrenia, or personality disorders.

It might also be the case that relevance is determined by the impact of having (or not having) the problem in question, in terms of treatment outcome. Generally, co-occurring psychiatric disorders have been found to be associated with negative outcomes, so knowing about their presence or absence would be of practical value in determining who may be at risk for treatment attrition, or less-than-average therapeutic benefit. Decisions about whether to refer, treat in collaboration with another provider, or render both addiction and mental health treatments "in-house" can then be based on data.

Psychometric Properties

The psychometric properties of a measuring instrument are important in making a selection. It is relatively easy to construct a questionnaire or a survey. One can list a number of statements and have a respondent answer each statement yes or no. Many popular magazines create such surveys; for example, you might take a quiz to discover your "Love IQ." While you might be entertained, you probably would not have any confidence in such a measure.

In contrast, clinicians must have confidence in the measures they use. Measuring tools should measure what they are supposed to measure, show some consistency in doing so, and relate in some significant way to the construct they are supposed to measure. Just as most people who purchase a car will never learn about its engine mechanics, most users of screening measures will pay little attention to the psychometrics.

For those who do, there are two types of psychometrics to consider: (1) sensitivity and specificity, and (2) reliability and validity. Both types of psychometrics are closely related.

Sensitivity and Specificity

To get an accurate measure, clinicians should try to eliminate "false-positive" and "false-negative" results. Sensitivity refers to the relative success of the measure at identifying the construct in question. A highly sensitive measure will identify people who have a disorder, but it also may falsely identify some people who do not have the disorder. Some depression measures produce higher sensitive estimates for a mood disorder; a clinician may be interested in a sensitive measure at intake so he or she can be conservative in following up on this result during a detailed assessment.

In contrast, specificity pertains not only to the correct identification of patients with a disorder but also to the correct identification of patients without the disorder. Specificity may be more challenging for instrument developers to achieve, but it is an important consideration when false positives (i.e., incorrectly identifying a case as having the disorder) are costly (such as in ordering unnecessary medical tests). With respect to co-occurring disorders, however, specificity may be important in correctly identifying more specific disorders such as PTSD or social anxiety disorder, which have a demonstrated risk for negative treatment outcomes.

Reliability and Validity

The other psychometric properties of screening measures are reliability and validity. Reliability pertains to the internal consistency of the instrument and the consistency across patients and over time. In other words, the measure should produce the same results on repeated screenings of the same patient under the same conditions. Validity, as the term implies, is the estimated relationship between the findings on the screening measure and objective findings, for example, via standardized and structured clinical interview. In other words, the assessment should accurately measure what the clinician set out to measure. Validity estimates pertain directly to the issue of sensitivity and specificity.

It is good to select a measure that has been developed by people who studied the measure's psychometric properties and reported these properties in a scientific journal. This is a professional way of helping users of the measure know its strengths and limitations as they consider its use.

Complexity and Cost

Additional things to think through when selecting a measure include its complexity and its cost. Some measures are lengthy (i.e., they take an hour to complete), and others are hard to read or difficult to administer. Short and simple should be the guidepost.

Screening measures differ in terms of cost. Public domain measures, sometimes developed by public officials under the auspices of federal grants or by academic department faculty, are free of charge. Sometimes permission is required, but often the only cost is for reproduction. Other measures are proprietary and marketed by testing corporations. Although the cost of most of these measures is relatively inexpensive (compared to a standard laboratory test, such as a urinalysis drug screen), many public sector agencies find any cost prohibitive.

The practitioner or program leader will need to evaluate a potential screening measure for these characteristics and, if he or she does so, will likely make an informed decision about which measures to implement.

Generic Screening Measures

Generic screening measures cover a broad range of psychiatric disorders in a relatively limited number of items. We have found two generic screening measures useful in assessing for psychiatric problems among patients with co-occurring disorders: the Modified Mini Screen (MMS) and the Mental Health Screening Form–III (MHSF–III). Both of these measures are more sensitive than specific, but the findings from both will trigger a more detailed assessment (or more specific screening) for a range of disorders.

The Modified Mini Screen (MMS) is a self-report measure that rapidly assesses for present mood, anxiety, and psychoticspectrum disorders. It can be completed quickly by most patients, and it is easily scored by either a clinician or support staff. Among patients with substance use disorders, a cutoff score of 6 is seen to be very sensitive to predicting the presence of psychiatric disorder, whereas the cutoff score of 9 is more specific. A copy of the MMS is included on the CD-ROM.

The Mental Health Screening Form–III (MHSF–III) is also a self-report measure that covers a range of disorders.

Modified Mini Screen (MMS)

- Self-report
- Screens for mood, anxiety, and psychotic disorders
- Twenty-two questions
- Yes/no format
- Fifteen minutes

Mental Health Screening Form–III (MHSF–III)

- Self-report or clinician-administered
- Screens for thirteen disorders
- Eighteen questions
- Yes/no format
- Quick to complete

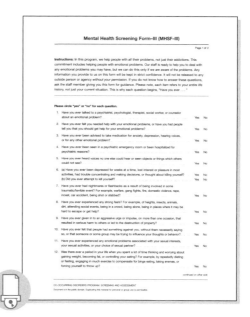

It can be completed relatively quickly and covers an even broader range of psychiatric disorders than the MMS. A copy of the MHSF–III is included on the CD-ROM.

In sum, the MMS and the MHSF–III are generic screening measures with certain advantages:

- They are frequently used.
- They are in the public domain.
- They are highly sensitive.
- They assess for the most common disorders that are co-morbid with substance use disorders.
- They are easily scored and administered.

Based on our experience, we favor the MMS because of its reported psychometric properties.

Two other generic screening measures for substance use disorders are included on the CD-ROM: the CAGE Adapted to Include Drugs (CAGE-AID) and the Simple Screening Instrument for Alcohol and Other Drugs (SSI-AOD).

The CAGE-AID is a sensitive screen for alcohol and drug problems. A copy of the CAGE-AID is included on the CD-ROM. "CAGE" is an acronym for

C - Ever try to **Cut back** on your drinking or drug use?

A - Ever been **Annoyed** by anyone about your drinking or drug use?

G - Ever felt **Guilty** or ashamed about your drinking or drug use?

E - Ever had an **"Eye-opener"** or used alcohol or drugs in the morning?

The SSI-AOD consists of sixteen questions and is more specific than the CAGE-AID. A copy of the SSI-AOD is included on the CD-ROM. Both measures are simple, reliable, valid, and in the public domain.

Specific Screening Measures for Mental Health Disorders

The same criteria to evaluate the potential of a generic screening measure should be applied to the selection of a specific screening measure. The added consideration in selecting a specific screening measure is the importance of *specificity*.

Based on the research of prevalence and associated negative outcomes for patients with co-occurring substance use disorders, we recommend specific screening measures for mood disorders, PTSD, and social phobia.

Although both bipolar disorder and antisocial and borderline personality disorders are common in addiction treatment, experts believe that these disorders are not reliably or accurately assessed using screening tools, particularly self-administered ones. A patient with bipolar disorder often lacks insight into the expansiveness and grandiosity associated with hypomanic symptoms (particularly during the manic phase); a patient with antisocial personality disorder may likewise lack awareness of the behaviors and relational patterns needed to meet diagnostic criteria. Similarly, borderline personality disorder is often reflected in elevated responses to screening measures for mood, anxiety, and PTSD; however, this disorder is often reliably assessed via clinical interview.

Mood Disorders

Unipolar mood disorders, including dysthymia and major depression, are the most common psychiatric disorders co-occurring with both alcohol and drug use disorders. Having a specific screening measure to assess for mood disorders, including acute symptoms such as suicide risk, is recommended for standardizing the potential to detect these disorders.

There are a number of self-report screening measures for depression. The following are the most commonly used:

- **Beck Depression Inventory (BDI)**
  The BDI, now in its second edition, is the most frequently used measure. It has twenty-one items. Cutoff scores of 20 (moderate) and 30 (severe) indicate depression. Two items are associated with suicide risk. A combined total on these two items is associated with acute risk.

- **Center for Epidemiologic Studies Depression Scale (CES-D Scale)**
  The CES-D Scale has twenty items about depressive symptoms. They are rated on a 4-point scale as to how many days the respondent was bothered by these symptoms over the past week. A total score of 60 is possible, though scores of 15 or greater (mild to moderate depression) and 21 or greater (major depression) are considered clinically significant.

- **Patient Health Questionnaire 9 (PHQ-9) and Hamilton Depression Scale**
  Both are common in studies of antidepressant medication. However, the PHQ-9 is proprietary, and the Hamilton is an expert clinician rating scale. These measures are similar in brevity, practicality, ease of administration and scoring, and psychometric properties.

- **Zung Self-Rating Depression Scale**
  The Zung is a twenty-item measure in the public domain. Symptoms of depression are rated on a 4-point scale, with several items noted positively so it can reduce or at least detect response bias. The maximum score is 80, though a score of 50 or above is considered clinically significant.

We recommend the CES-D Scale as a specific screening measure for depression among patients with substance use problems. It has excellent psychometric properties, is easy to administer and score, and is in the public domain. You can find a copy of the CES-D Scale on the CD-ROM. See pages 87–89 of the clinician's guide for information on how to obtain the other screening materials mentioned here.

Anxiety Disorders

Next to unipolar mood disorders, anxiety is the most common disorder among patients with substance use disorders. As noted in chapter 2, feelings of anxiety, such as fear and worry, and symptoms of anxiety, such as in withdrawal and intoxication, are different from an anxiety disorder. Characteristics of anxiety disorders include irrational fear, avoidance, and impaired functioning. Screening for anxiety disorders makes good clinical practice; thus, including a specific measure to assess for the potential presence or absence of an anxiety disorder is warranted.

Although there are several measures for all of the *DSM-5* anxiety disorders, the two most common are the Beck Anxiety Inventory (BAI) and the Hamilton Anxiety Scale. Both have good psychometric properties. The Hamilton Anxiety Scale is in the public domain and may be reproduced without permission. Like the Hamilton Depression Scale, the Hamilton Anxiety Scale requires expert clinician rating, so the BAI is favorable because of its potential for self-report.

The BAI consists of twenty-one items rated on a 4-point scale from 1 (Not at all) to 4 (Severely). The maximum score is 84; scores of 16 or more (Moderate) or 26 or more (Severe) are considered clinically significant. Like the Beck Depression Inventory, the BAI is proprietary. See pages 87–89 of the clinician's guide for information on how to obtain these screening materials.

PTSD

PTSD and social anxiety are two specific disorders with particular clinical significance in addiction treatment settings, and as co-morbid with substance use disorders, they merit specific screening approaches. Also, in the analysis by Barlow (2002), they were consistently found to predate the onset of substance use and, accordingly, are most likely independent rather than substance-induced anxiety disorders. For this reason, we recommend specific screening for these two disorders.

PTSD, or post-traumatic stress disorder, is common among persons with substance use disorders. It is more common among women than men, and it is associated with more intense addictive substances, more severe substance-related problems, other psychiatric impairment, and a host of other negative correlates. PTSD is also a risk for treatment attrition, for more frequent relapse to substances, and, co-existing with substance use, for less improvement in PTSD symptoms. Unlike with other anxiety disorders, clinicians recognize the unique aspects to PTSD and note the profound trauma in patients' backgrounds. Further, somewhat unique among anxiety disorders, the presence of re-experiencing symptoms such as nightmares, flashbacks, and intrusive thoughts and memories makes PTSD more clinically troubling than other disorders (McGovern et al. 2008).

Despite considerable interest in improving services for woman and for patients with PTSD, many providers continue to confuse trauma with PTSD. Trauma is a negative life event. *DSM-5* lists a variety of types of such events as part of "Criterion A" for PTSD, also specifying the means of exposure—for example, whether the person directly experienced it, witnessed it, or learned about it. However, the experience of trauma has not been demonstrated to be associated with negative treatment response, and for this reason, screening for trauma alone may not be relevant.

For a PTSD diagnosis, a person must have experienced an A-Criterion traumatic life event, and also several other criteria: Criterion B describes the symptoms' intrusiveness (re-experiencing the trauma), C describes avoidance of the symptoms' triggers, D specifies negative changes in cognition or mood, and E describes changes in the person's levels of arousal and activity. In contrast to persons with only a trauma, persons with PTSD are at increased risk for negative outcomes. Therefore, screening for PTSD is relevant.

Screening for PTSD necessitates two detection components: (1) the experience of a traumatic life event, and (2) symptoms of re-experiencing, avoidance, negative changes in cognition or mood, and hyper-arousal that interfere with functioning. To this end, we recommend using both the Life Events Checklist and the PTSD Checklist (PCL).

The Life Events Checklist is part of the Clinician-Administered PTSD Scale (CAPS) published by Western Psychological Services. For each event in the Life Events Checklist, the patient indicates whether he or she has experienced it, witnessed it, learned about it, or it doesn't apply. The PCL focuses on the patient's

Duplicating this page is illegal. Do not copy this material without written permission from the publisher.

39

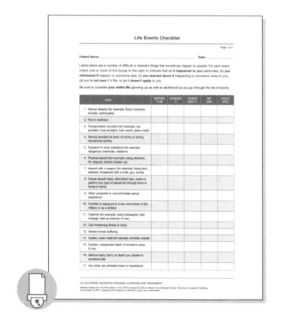
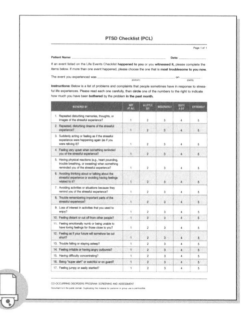

most troublesome event. The PTSD symptoms are rated on a 5-point scale from 1 (Not at all) to 5 (Extremely). Scores of 44 or more are associated with a diagnosis of PTSD.

Copies of the Life Events Checklist and the PCL are included on the CD-ROM.

Social Anxiety Disorder

Much like PTSD, social anxiety disorder is common among persons with substance use disorders and associated with negative outcomes. Perhaps the most negative of outcomes is the fact that persons with social anxiety disorder are unlikely to access any formal treatment, emblematic of the psychiatric disorder from which they suffer—avoidance of social situations. In particular, since it is common knowledge that much of traditional addiction treatment occurs in group formats, many persons with social phobia will seek other avenues to deal with co-occurring substance use and social anxiety disorder.

Recent data from the National Co-morbidity Survey of over eight thousand U.S. adults (Kessler, Stein, and Berglund 1998) found high rates of social anxiety disorder in the population (5 percent to 10 percent), and about half had co-occurring substance use disorders. This finding was replicated in a larger sample of over forty thousand U.S. adults (Grant et al. 2004). Interestingly, Kessler also distinguished between persons with social anxiety disorder and those with more pervasive social fears. The latter group was termed to suffer from more generalized "social anxiety." These persons suffered greater impairment and more avoidance, and they were more likely to have co-occurring substance use disorders. Our own research finds that social anxiety is common in addiction treatment settings (20 percent to 30 percent) and associated with treatment dropout. For this reason, assessing for social anxiety is warranted and relevant.

One measure, the Social Interaction Anxiety Scale (SIAS), is in the public domain and has been used with persons having substance-related disorders. The SIAS is a twenty-item, self-report measure in which respondents rate their distress about specific social interactions on a 5-point scale from 0 (Not at all characteristic of me) to 4 (Extremely characteristic of me). A total score of 60 is possible with cutoffs of 34 or more (social phobia) and 43 or more (social anxiety) designated as clinically significant.

The SIAS is easily completed and relatively simple to score and interpret. A copy is included on the CD-ROM.

Specific Screening Measures for Substance Use Disorders

The most accurate, specific screening measures for alcohol and drug use disorders are objective screens of urine, breath, or hair samples. For alcohol problems, breath samples are most reliable and valid. For drugs, urine samples are most reliable and valid. Breathalyzer devices are commercially available and can be reused (with disposable mouthpieces) to detect estimates of blood-alcohol concentration.

Urinalysis kits are also commercially available and can detect for a panel of substances including opioids, cocaine, cannabis, amphetamine/methamphetamine, and benzodiazepines/barbiturates/anxiolytics. These test kits can be purchased for about five dollars per use. Urinalyses via chain-of-custody assays to toxicology laboratories are available in most areas. Many hospital laboratories, particularly those with occupational medicine departments, can conduct analyses for the most common drugs of abuse. Laboratory processing of urine samples is particularly important for clients who are mandated to treatment, or when positive findings have implications beyond the treatment settings. For most treatment purposes, the urine test kits are adequate. Hair sample analysis is expensive and generally used only in cases where there is suspicion of episodic and concealed use of drugs, and for which forensic-quality verification is necessary.

Although urine and breath samples are not considered biohazardous materials, many mental health providers resist the implementation of these measures in their practice. Providers admit that they are uncomfortable with the "bodily fluid" aspect to these approaches, but they also mention concerns about violations of patient boundaries and trust. These issues are more typically encountered in practices that lean toward the psychodynamic, individual therapy approaches. Addiction treatment providers have extensive experience in managing therapeutic relationships while obtaining objective screening measures. In general, the staff member obtaining the sample is not the patient's individual therapist. There is also a requirement that someone of the same sex obtain the sample. For the quick-test kits, no direct observation is necessary (unlike urine samples for laboratory processing or samples involving chain-of-custody requirements for forensic purposes). Breath samples are obtained in the office.

Patients often see, retrospectively, objective indicators of specific substance use as the most important factor in their early treatment experience. In long-term studies of physicians in recovery, the physicians reported that urine monitoring was probably the most helpful measure in securing their early sobriety. In response to the typical patient retort of "Don't you trust me to tell you?" many addiction treatment providers say, "Of course, we trust you; this just verifies it for us both."

For more information on Breathalyzers and quick-test kits, visit the following Web sites:

- www.breathalyzer.net
- http://alcotester.com
- www.breathalyzersonline.com
- www.toxassociates.com/alcohol.htm
- www.medicaldisposables.us

Also, Hazelden publishes a series of manuals on drug testing. *Drug Testing in Treatment Settings* is helpful for inpatient and outpatient treatment facilities that use drug testing as a component in a comprehensive treatment program. *Drug Testing in Correctional Settings* provides guidance in using drug testing in criminal justice settings, including prisons, jails, community corrections, and parole.

How to Use the Screening Measures Provided on the CD-ROM

In systematic and standardized screening for co-occurring psychiatric disorders among persons with substance use disorders, we recommend starting with the Modified Mini Screen (MMS). As noted, the MMS is a *sensitive generic screening* measure that will detect a broad range of psychiatric problems. It is included as the first-line screening measure on the CD-ROM. (For a thumbnail view, see page 35.)

If a person scores a 6 or more on the MMS, or more conservatively scores a 9 or above, you can screen for more specific disorders that have negative treatment implications if they are present: mood disorders, PTSD, and social anxiety disorder. However, even if a patient does not score above either of these thresholds, the clinician should examine further any positively endorsed symptoms. More specific screening measures will identify the presence or absence of these important disorders. Figure 10 reviews specific screening measures for co-occurring psychiatric disorders.

FIGURE 10

Specific Screening Measures for Co-occurring Psychiatric Disorders

If a patient scores a 6 or more on the Modified Mini Screen (MMS), you can screen for more specific disorders using the measure(s) indicated in the chart. These screening measures are provided on the CD-ROM.

PROBLEM/DISORDER	MEASURES
Mood Disorders	Center for Epidemiologic Studies Depression Scale (CES-D Scale)
Trauma/PTSD	Life Events Checklist and PTSD Checklist (PCL)
Social Anxiety Disorder	Social Interaction Anxiety Scale (SIAS)

If patients score above the cutoff threshold in the specific screening measure, then the clinician must carefully begin to assess for the presence of these disorders. Even if patients do not score above these indicated thresholds, the patient is well served to have the clinician inquire about these symptoms.

By implementing generic and specific screening measures, you will increase your capacity to detect co-occurring psychiatric problems among persons with substance use disorders. These screening measures are the first step in the initial clinical process of assessment. Findings from these measures must be interpreted by a clinician and, in and of themselves, do not yield conclusive data. Nevertheless, by using these measures, you will increase the consistency of your approach to your patients' care and potentially increase their chances of recovery. ▼

KEY POINTS ADDRESSED IN CHAPTER 4

1. Screening measures can be selected based on relevance, psychometric properties, complexity, and cost.

2. Generic screening measures are sensitive to detecting a range of psychiatric problems. The Modified Mini Screen (MMS) is an example of one such screening measure.

3. Specific screening measures are deployed when greater specificity is necessary in detecting the presence of a disorder of particular clinical significance. The CES-D, PCL, and SIAS are examples of these types of measures.

The Assessment and Diagnostic Process

What Is Assessment?

Assessment is the process of strategically gathering information from a patient in order to ascertain the presence or absence of a disorder. In addition, assessment involves determining the protective and risk factors associated with this patient at this point in time. A patient's motivation for change and professional help, and degree of present risk to self or others, may be components of the assessment package. Finally, an assessment should also focus on developing the treatment plan: How can you help this individual?

This chapter will focus on establishing or ruling out the presence of a co-occurring psychiatric disorder among patients with substance use disorders. Although the outcome of an assessment may not necessarily yield a formal diagnosis, it will certainly advance clinical precision in identifying, beyond the screening process, if a psychiatric disorder is likely present.

Essentially, there are two goals in assessment for co-occurring psychiatric disorders: (1) establishing or ruling out a psychiatric diagnosis, and (2) using the data from the assessment to develop a treatment plan.

Methods of Assessment

Several methods are used in assessing for psychiatric disorders or problems among people with substance use disorders. These are

- structured clinical interview using standardized measures
- self-report measures
- clinical interview

Duplicating this page is illegal. Do not copy this material without written permission from the publisher.

45

Structured Clinical Interview Using Standardized Measures

Among the best-known structured clinical interviews are the following:

- Structured Clinical Interview for *DSM-IV* (SCID) by the American Psychiatric Association

- Composite International Diagnostic Interview (CIDI) by the World Health Organization

- Mini International Neuropsychiatric Interview (MINI) by David Sheehan and Yves Lecrubier

- Psychiatric Research Interview for Substance and Mental Disorders (PRISM) by Deborah Hasin and colleagues

- Alcohol Use Disorder and Associated Disabilities Interview Schedule (AUDADIS) by Bridget Grant and colleagues

- Global Appraisal of Individual Needs (GAIN) by Chestnut Health Systems

- Addiction Severity Index (ASI) by A. T. McLellan, L. Luborski, J. Cacciola, P. McGrahan, and P. O'Brien

The SCID, CIDI, PRISM, AUDADIS, and MINI are designed to establish formal diagnosis. Intensive training is required for the SCID, CIDI, PRISM, and AUDADIS, and for this reason their use is primarily confined to research. The MINI is briefer and easier to use, and it requires much less formal training.

Both the ASI and the GAIN are in widespread use across the United States. The ASI was first used in the 1980s and has undergone a number of revisions. The ASI does not detail diagnoses, but instead develops composite measures for life problems, including psychiatric problems. As such, although it is an excellent measure to assess problems and outcomes, it is not the best measure to establish or rule out psychiatric disorders. However, the ASI is the only one of these seven assessment measures that is in the public domain.

Many community providers across the country have adopted the GAIN, mainly because the Center for Substance Abuse Treatment (CSAT) mandates its use in multisite studies of adolescent services. Another factor in its popularity is that the GAIN has established reliability and validity for adolescents, and it can also be used with adults. Much like the ASI, the GAIN is more of a measure of problems associated with substance use. However, the GAIN also derives scores on symptom problem scales. These problem scales have been found to be associated with a series of issues including depression, anxiety, trauma, attention deficit hyperactivity disorder, and conduct and thought disorders. Much like the SCID, CIDI, PRISM, and

AUDADIS, the GAIN also requires intensive training and, relative to other measures, is perhaps the most expensive to use. See pages 87–89 for information on how to obtain the GAIN.

The SCID, CIDI, PRISM, AUDADIS, and ASI were reviewed in 2007 and their strengths and weaknesses described (Samet et al. 2007). Treatment provider response to this review highlighted the inherent difficulties in using the SCID, CIDI, PRISM, and AUDADIS in real world clinical settings, and noted instead the utility of these formal measures for research purposes (Blaine, Forman, and Svikis 2007).

Self-Report Measures

Self-report diagnostic measures exist, such as the Psychiatric Diagnostic Screening Questionnaire (PDSQ) by Mark Zimmerman, but they are probably more like screening measures than diagnostic instruments. Often-cited problems with this format include length of measure and time of administration, as well as serious concerns about accuracy, especially for people with severe disorders.

Clinical Interview

By far the most common approach to establishing diagnosis and contributing to a treatment plan is the clinical interview. Formal assessments are core aspects of curriculum for psychiatrists, psychologists, social workers, mental health counselors, and addiction counselors. The training focus for these disciplines might vary, but all treatment professionals learn some key dimensions, and approaches, for assessing those people seeking their consultation.

Assessment for Common Psychiatric Disorders

Assessment in addiction treatment historically has involved a "bio-psycho-social" approach, with a primary focus on substance use disorders. Patients are asked about the substances they have used, the age of first use, the frequency and amount of use, and potential consequences and symptoms. Prior treatment experiences, the level of care, and treatment responses are also noted. Social factors assessed consist of family of origin and development, current living situation (supports and risks), housing, and work functioning. Medical problem assessment often consists of a review of potential disorders, with a series of checks if present. Over the past decade, infectious diseases, including HIV/AIDS and hepatitis C, are frequently more thoroughly assessed. Little emphasis has been placed on the "psycho" aspect. Except for an inquiry about previous diagnoses, treatments, and current risk for suicide, a limited amount of psychological data was gathered, and hardly any in a formal or systematic manner.

We have provided forms that outline the assessment process for the most common psychiatric disorders in addiction treatment: major depression, persistent depressive disorder, anxiety disorders such as social anxiety disorder, PTSD, and manic/hypomanic/bipolar disorder. Also, because suicide is of particular concern for persons with co-occurring disorders, we have included a form for suicidality. These forms are adaptations of the MINI 5.0 but are substantially different because they feature filters for intoxication, withdrawal, and substance-induced versus independent disorders. These clinical assessment forms can be found on the CD-ROM. (A sample thumbnail view is shown here.) The purpose of these forms is to provide structure to the assessment process and to add to the establishment or rule-out of a psychiatric disorder within the appropriate scope of practice.

A clinician can use the data obtained during screening (see chapter 4) to identify the potential presence of a disorder, or at least a suspicion. On the clinical assessment form, each symptom is marked either yes or no, and then the data are subjected to filters to rule out (1) intoxication or withdrawal and (2) substance-induced disorders. If the symptoms are found to exist, even after considering the alternative explanations in (1) and (2), then a more formal diagnostic process (by a person who can diagnose within his or her scope of practice) and/or the development of a treatment plan are the next steps.

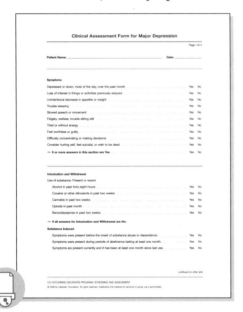

These clinical assessment forms do not substitute for an in-depth clinical interview by a licensed clinician. However, the list of symptoms and filters can assist the trained clinician and the nonlicensed counselor in focusing on specific disorders both for their presence and for their inclusion on the treatment plan.

The filters for intoxication or withdrawal are rough guidelines based on the effects of particular substances (see chapter 2). The filter for substance-induced disorder is based on the differential diagnostic framework of the *DSM-5*. Some disorders, for example, PTSD, are not categorized as substance-induced, whereas others (major depression, anxiety, bipolar disorder) may be highly subject to the effects of substances and substance use disorders.

These assessment guides can augment either a structured or unstructured clinical interview by either a licensed or unlicensed professional.

Diagnosis

The forms will guide the assessment process toward clarity in determining diagnoses. A licensed professional must make formal diagnoses, but counselors and other supervised clinical staff members can indicate more precise and continued rule-outs. Further, it will be important for all staff to understand the differences between intoxication and withdrawal symptoms, substance-induced disorders, and independent psychiatric disorders.

A formal diagnosis will take into account the time periods as defined in the *DSM-5* (over the past year, past six months, past month, and so on) to meet criteria for a specific diagnosis at present.

Some diagnoses may not be present but may have been true at some point in the patient's life. For example, a person who meets criteria for lifetime PTSD but over the past year has not been symptomatic does not meet criteria for current (or past thirty days) PTSD. Of course, having had any disorder at some point in life is a risk factor for the disorder at present (or in the near future) even if the patient does not meet criteria.

The process of "monitoring, monitoring, monitoring" and "assessing, assessing, assessing" cannot be overemphasized.

Personality Disorders

This guide does not outline the criteria for personality disorders, two of which are common among people with substance use disorders: antisocial personality and borderline personality disorder. Clinicians are referred to the *DSM-5* and to the Structured Clinical Interview for *DSM-IV* (SCID) created by the American Psychiatric Association for the criteria for assessing and diagnosing these disorders. We chose not to feature them in this guide because of lack of diagnostic precision and reliability and difficulty in establishing these diagnoses among people who are either actively using substances or who just recently discontinued use.

What to Do Next?

It is essential to use the findings from the assessment as the basis of the treatment plan. Disorders should be the focal goals of the treatment plan. Treatments and interventions, whether pharmacological or psychosocial, have been developed for and are targeted at specific diagnosed disorders.

In chapter 7, we organize the assessment and diagnostic "data" into the treatment and recovery plan. But first, we must discuss a critical and often-overlooked aspect to treatment of people with co-occurring disorders: patient stage of motivation and readiness for treatment. ▼

KEY POINTS ADDRESSED IN CHAPTER

5

1. Assessment is a thorough and detailed review of symptoms and their chronology to determine the presence or absence of a co-occurring psychiatric disorder and to develop a treatment plan.

2. The most common assessment methods are structured clinical interviews, self-report, and unstructured clinical interviews.

3. When making a differential diagnosis for independent psychiatric problems, clinicians must consider substance intoxication and withdrawal and rule out the *DSM-5* criteria for substance-induced disorders.

Assessing Motivation

KEY QUESTIONS RAISED IN CHAPTER 6:

1. Why is it important to assess patient motivation?

2. What aspects of motivation should be assessed?

3. Can I assess a patient's motivation to address both substance use *and* psychiatric issues?

Stages of Change

The research work of James Prochaska and Carlo DiClemente, as clinically put into operation by Miller and colleagues, changed the landscape of treatment for both mental health and psychiatric disorders. The detail and scope of this work will not be reviewed here. The major principles involve a more humanistic, patient-centered approach, awareness that motivation to change behavior is important to the clinical process, and conceptualizing motivation in a series of stages. Miller and Rollnick's work (motivational interviewing) is adapted in the curriculum *Integrating Combined Therapies for People with Co-occurring Disorders,* and a refinement of their approach for patients with co-occurring disorders is a component of that guide.

There are two well-known measures of the stages of change created by Prochaska and DiClemente. These are the SOCRATES (Stages of Change Readiness and Treatment Eagerness Scale) and the URICA (University of Rhode Island Change Assessment) scale. Both measures are in the public domain and are widely used in treatment programs.

The stages of change are primarily a cognitive-behavioral model. For simplicity, this guide will be utilizing a four-stage version of the stages of change.

Precontemplation: I do not have a problem.

Contemplation: I may have a problem, but am not sure.

Action: I am initiating changes.

Maintenance: I have made changes and am trying to sustain them.

These stages form the basis of motivational interviewing (MI) and motivational enhancement therapy (MET), namely, targeting interventions in a deliberate but nondirective way, and leveraging patient motivation by an awareness of the

Duplicating this page is illegal. Do not copy this material without written permission from the publisher.

51

stage of readiness. Patients at the Precontemplation stage need information to connect with the possible reason for change. Weighing the pros and cons of changing or not changing characterizes MI interventions at the Contemplation stage. "Rolling with resistance" versus confrontation is a key dimension to the treatment approach at this stage.

The Action stage is where much of MI leaves off. At this juncture other interventions, such as cognitive-behavioral therapy (CBT), frequently are more appropriate. For this reason many clinicians combine MI and CBT early on in psychosocial treatments. A Center for Substance Abuse Treatment (CSAT) manual for adolescent substance abuse using MET/CBT has been developed and tested and is now an evidence-based practice for youth with substance use disorders (Sampl and Kadden 2001, 2002).

The Maintenance stage is perhaps the primary focus of traditional addiction treatment and is perhaps the primary purpose of peer recovery support groups. (For example, from the Alcoholics Anonymous preamble: "Our primary purpose is to stay sober and to help other alcoholics [addicts] to achieve sobriety.") For patients at this stage, relapse prevention should be the main focus and is exactly what patients at this stage seek.

The evidence for the efficacy of the stages of change and MI approach to patients with substance use disorders is overwhelmingly convincing. Addressing motivation and tailoring treatment response is associated with treatment retention and more positive substance use outcomes. Clinical anecdote suggests this to be an easier and kinder approach to take with patients, and MI/MET probably is among the most widely adopted evidence-based practices (McGovern et al. 2004; DiClemente, Nidecker, and Bellack 2008).

The stages of change model has some critics. These critics point out that the stages of change do not take into account

- the rapid changes forward and back in patient motivation
- the difficulty in determining the time frame to assess the stage (over the past hour, past week, past month)
- differential motivation for different substances (e.g., heroin versus cocaine or alcohol)
- the validity of patient beliefs or attitudes about motivation (versus actual demonstrated behavior)
- the fact that persons can be at different stages for different reasons (internal versus external factors)

- the length and complexity of scales designed to measure the stages (see screening measures, chapter 4)

Few clinicians have fundamental reservations about the stages of change as a model, but many practitioners have noted the limitations of its practical application. Further, more comprehensive stages of change models have not been applied to patients with co-occurring disorders, who may be at different levels of motivation to address substance use versus a psychiatric problem. For this reason, many clinicians utilize a simple approach to assessing patient motivation to change either the substance use or mental health problems, as well as patient confidence in making the change. These can be put on motivational "rulers" (much like patient ratings or pain measures) as seen in figure 11. This figure shows an example of a self-report measure to assess patient motivation.

FIGURE 11

Simple Patient Self-Report Questionnaire

On a 10-point scale, how much do you want to change your substance use now?

Not at all   1   2   3   4   5   6   7   8   9   10   Totally

On a 10-point scale, how sure are you that you will be able to make this change?

Not at all   1   2   3   4   5   6   7   8   9   10   Totally

On a 10-point scale, how much do you want to change your mental health problem?

Not at all   1   2   3   4   5   6   7   8   9   10   Totally

On a 10-point scale, how sure are you that you will be able to make this change?

Not at all   1   2   3   4   5   6   7   8   9   10   Totally

Stage of Treatment

The stages of change model has focused primarily on the motivation to change a behavior, not so much on beliefs about the need for professional treatment. Thus, a person could be at the Action stage of motivation ("I want to stop drinking") but not be willing to seek help or take the necessary steps to be successful in this undertaking. In traditional Twelve Step recovery philosophy, this unwillingness might indicate that the person has not taken Step One (Admitted we were powerless and that our lives had become unmanageable). In this case a person may be motivated to address substance use based on its unmanageability, but unwilling to admit the need for outside help. This discrepancy (motivation to change versus motivation for help or treatment) is crucial and important to assess.

Further, there is often a discrepancy between what a person involved in a change process says or believes and what he or she does. The person who wishes to stop drinking may have the best of intentions, but unless he or she takes active steps and does so consistently and over time, his or her chances for recovery are not favorable.

Several other issues distinguish the motivation for change from the motivation for help.

Tendency to Minimize Severity of Addiction

It is not uncommon for persons suffering from substance use disorders to make daily vows, public and private, to stop using. At the nadir of a hangover or in the throes of the consequences of a cocaine binge, the alcoholic or addict will exclaim in all sincerity: "Never again." These promises, violated to oneself and others, constitute the definition of addiction: loss of control. Nonetheless, when only desire and intent to stop substance use are addressed, the loss-of-control issue is overlooked.

Stating Intentions versus Taking Steps

Most motivational measures assess behavioral intention, beliefs, or attitudes, but not behavior. Stating an intention and actually taking the necessary steps (i.e., changing one's social network, taking a medication, attending peer recovery support group meetings) are very different from simply expressing one's intentions, beliefs, or attitudes. In other words, it's the difference between "Talking the talk" and "Walking the talk."

Shifting Back and Forth between Stages

Most clinicians have observed a patient who demonstrates little motivation or is in Precontemplation at best. During the course of a session, the clinician may help the patient make connections between his or her life problems and substances. By the end of the session, the patient may be more willing to address the addiction and understands the consequences of the disease. Apparently the patient has shifted from Precontemplation to Action. However, when the patient arrives for a session the following week, the clinician quickly learns that the patient seems no longer at the Action stage but seems back to Precontemplation.

The cognitive aspects of motivation change. Patient motivation drifts from week to week, day to day, and, sometimes, within the context of a fifty-minute session. What should be the time frame for an assessment of motivation: now, over the past week, the past two weeks, the past month? These parameters must be considered when assessing patient motivation.

Fewer Measures Available

SOCRATES and URICA, the best-known and best-researched measures for patient motivation, assess primarily the cognitive aspects of motivation, not the behavioral. These measures are excellent for assisting in the recognition of the patient's appreciation of the nature of his or her problem and what the intentions for change may be.

In response to these issues, our group developed the Substance Abuse Treatment Scale (SATS). The SATS focuses on *treatment behavior,* not cognition. It also has stages, but they are based on actions the patient takes and are measured over a "past-month" time frame. There are several versions of the SATS; one with four stages is provided on the CD-ROM.

A four-stage version is as follows:

Engagement: Person is not using treatment.

Persuasion: Person is attending treatment but is not participating because he or she either does not see a problem or does not see treatment as the solution.

Active: Person is attending treatment and working with a provider to change.

Relapse Prevention: Person has benefited from Active treatment and is working with a provider less intensively to maintain gains and prevent relapse.

The SATS treatment behavior stages correspond to and fit nicely with the stages of change model for motivation cognitions (see figure 12 on page 56).

The stages of change and the SATS models focus exclusively on substance use thoughts and behaviors, respectively. Persons with co-occurring disorders may be at different stages with respect to changing substance use than they are with mental health concerns.

One patient may define his problem as alcoholism but be reluctant if not belligerent when it is suggested that a related problem is PTSD from his experience as a U.S. soldier in Iraq. He may be at an Action/Active stage for alcohol use, but a Contemplation/Persuasion stage for PTSD.

Duplicating this page is illegal. Do not copy this material without written permission from the publisher.

55

FIGURE 12

Stage-wise Treatment

STAGES OF CHANGE	STAGES OF TREATMENT
• Precontemplation	• Engagement
• Contemplation	• Persuasion
• Action	• Active
• Maintenance	• Relapse Prevention

A patient who has sought help from her primary care physician and her private psychiatrist for depression may now be in addiction treatment because of an impaired driving offense (as a result of her addiction to benzodiazepines). She may be at a Maintenance/Relapse Prevention stage with respect to her mood disorder, and at the Precontemplation/Engagement stage regarding her dependence on clonazepam. Therefore, in dealing with persons who have co-occurring disorders, assessing motivation to address both substance use and the psychiatric issue is essential. Likewise, as with substance use disorders alone, it is important not only to assess cognition but also behavior. The answer to these needs is a two-by-two scale that assesses cognitive *and* behavioral readiness for treatment for substance use problems *and* mental health problems. The scale is the Stage of Motivation and Treatment Readiness for Co-occurring Disorders (SOMTR-COD).

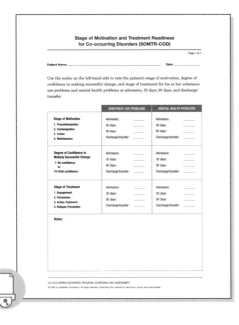

The SOMTR-COD is included on the CD-ROM. It is a simple measure to be completed by the clinician. It rates patient cognition and behavior using a global rating on the four stages of the stages of change model and the four stages of the SATS. Ratings are based on clinician impressions of patient communication and actual behavior on admission, at thirty days, at ninety days, and at discharge. As noted above, ratings are made for both substance use (including all substances) and mental health disorders/diagnoses (not problems).

A final rating is made on the patient's estimated confidence in the success of his or her change plan. This is known as a perceived "self-efficacy" rating.

Summary

Assessing patient motivation and the associated treatment behavior reflecting this motivation is critical. For patients with co-occurring disorders, motivation may vary by substance use and psychiatric disorder. Therefore, assessing each of these permutations, and making the assessment and stages transparent, is useful to guide a treatment process.

The next chapter on treatment planning details how to use this information in your conversations with patients. ▼

KEY POINTS ADDRESSED IN CHAPTER 6	1. Addressing patient motivation is important because it is associated with treatment retention and outcomes.
	2. Assessing both motivational beliefs and demonstrated treatment behaviors is recommended.
	3. Motivational beliefs and treatment behaviors for both substance use and psychiatric problems should be systematically assessed.

Duplicating this page is illegal. Do not copy this material without written permission from the publisher.

57

Developing a Recovery Plan

KEY QUESTIONS RAISED IN CHAPTER 7:

1. What key problem areas for patients with co-occurring disorders should I identify on a recovery plan?

2. What objectives and goals are important for treatment?

3. How do treatment provider capacity and patient motivation factor into developing the recovery plan?

Recovery Planning for Patients with Substance Use Disorders

The various approaches to addiction treatment planning and the regulatory requirements that may be necessary to develop a formal treatment plan are beyond the scope of this guide. Several manuals have been created for this specific purpose, including *The Addiction Treatment Planner* by Robert R. Perkinson, edited by Arthur E. Jongsma Jr. In addition, we advise providers, either at the program or individual practice level, to consult with their local, state, and professional licensure requirements for treatment or recovery plans.

With these caveats in mind, we acknowledge that treatment plans often are the bane of the practitioner's existence. A treatment plan is often perceived to artificially force a rather dynamic and artful, if not unpredictable, process into something architectural or engineered. It is as if human nature could be subject to blueprints for walls and windows.

Nevertheless, treatment plans are required, and they do afford the practitioner and program an opportunity to map a course and target a treatment toward a patient's specific problems. Further, a treatment plan provides the practitioner and patient with a document or living contract about the goals of the relationship. Put in this perspective, the treatment plan may be the best place to make explicit what patient and provider are doing together.

Most treatment or recovery plans consist of several core components:

- problem
- goal
- objective
- intervention

- responsible staff member
- target date

These components are often listed on a matrix (see the Comprehensive Recovery Plan for Patient with Co-occurring Disorders on the CD-ROM; a thumbnail view is on page 63). For electronic medical records, these components are often retained in a series of drop-down menus and "dictionaries" with long lists of possible goals, objectives, and interventions.

Historically, addiction treatment focused on simple goals for complicated people. The problem was "alcoholism," the goal was "sobriety," the objective was "abstinence," and the intervention was "working the Steps," particularly Steps One, Two, and Three. The responsible party was the primary counselor, and the target date could be as rapid as one week in a detoxification program, or one month in a traditional residential program.

Times have changed.

For addiction treatment providers focused on substance use disorders, the American Society of Addiction Medicine's third edition of its *Patient Placement Criteria (ASAM PPC-3)* provides six dimensions, which can be used not only to develop an assessment and rationale for patient placement, but also to develop goals and objectives. With respect to substance use disorders, the practitioner may consider the ASAM dimensions within the list of goals and objectives. The ASAM dimensions can be seen on the next page.

In assessing a patient along each of these dimensions for risk and for resources, the practitioner may also consider specific treatment goals and objectives. This provides a greater level of detail than providers have historically tracked. The Hazelden publication and DVD *Applying ASAM Placement Criteria* by David Mee-Lee (2007) can provide more information.

Recovery Planning for Persons with Co-occurring Disorders

Once the process of screening, assessment, and differential diagnosis has been completed, the treatment plan is ready for consideration. You have found patients with a "likely presence" of a psychiatric disorder co-existing with a substance use disorder.

You need to list each disorder identified through the assessment process on the treatment plan, regardless of whether you or your program plans on treating it. If your program lacks capacity to treat the disorder, you will need to alert another provider to the fact that the disorder exists. If the primary goal is to treat substance use issues, then the psychiatric problems must still be addressed as "complications" to recovery (see *ASAM PPC-3* Dimension 3: Emotional, Behavioral, or Cognitive Conditions and Complications).

What kind of interventions might you list to target the psychiatric problem? Here is a list of possible interventions:

- stabilization
- patient education about the disorder and treatment options
- assessing, monitoring, and working with patient motivation for change and treatment
- coping skills
- illness management and recovery skills
- medications

All people with psychiatric disorders can benefit from interventions such as these. Figure 13 on the following page shows a recovery plan for a person who screened positive on the Center for Epidemiologic Studies Depression Scale (CES-D Scale) and who was assessed to likely have a major depressive disorder.

ASAM Patient Placement Criteria

1. **Acute Intoxication and/or Withdrawal Potential**
   Risk associated with the patient's current level of acute intoxication; current signs of withdrawal; significant risk for severe symptoms or seizures upon withdrawal based on previous withdrawal history or current use patterns.

2. **Biomedical Conditions and Complications**
   The patient's current chronic medical conditions or physical illnesses (other than withdrawal) that may complicate treatment.

3. **Emotional, Behavioral, or Cognitive Conditions and Complications**
   The patient's current psychiatric disorders—behavioral, emotional, or cognitive—that may complicate treatment; chronic conditions; addictive disorders that require mental health treatment; ability to deal with activities of daily living.

4. **Readiness to Change**
   The patient's awareness of the need to change; level of commitment and readiness for change; likelihood to cooperate with treatment; recognition of the negative consequences of alcohol and/or drug use.

5. **Relapse/Continued Use, Continued Problem Potential**
   The patient's potential for relapse or continued use; ability of the patient to identify his or her relapse triggers; the patient's coping skills.

6. **Recovery/Living Environment**
   Family members, significant others, and living, work, and school environments that may pose a threat to treatment or recovery; issues such as child care, housing, employment, or transportation that may pose a threat to treatment or recovery; availability of supportive friends or financial, educational, and vocational resources to assist in treatment or recovery.

FIGURE 13

Sample Psychiatric Disorder Section of a
Comprehensive Recovery Plan

PROBLEM	GOAL	OBJECTIVE	INTERVENTION	RESPONSIBLE STAFF MEMBER	TARGET DATE
Major depression	Stabilize and initiate treatment	Ongoing monitoring for diagnostic accuracy	Weekly assessment		
		Patient education	Patient education group		
		Motivation	Motivational enhancement therapy (MET) for co-occurring disorders		
		Coping skills	Cognitive-behavioral therapy (CBT) for co-occurring disorders		
		Illness management and recovery skills	Twelve Step facilitation (TSF) for co-occurring disorders		
		Symptom management	Medication management		
		Family and social support	Family education and group therapy		

The interventions listed in figure 13 are available in the following components of the Co-occurring Disorders Program:

- Weekly assessment: *Screening and Assessment for People with Co-occurring Disorders*

- Motivational enhancement therapy (MET), cognitive-behavioral therapy (CBT), and Twelve Step facilitation (TSF): *Integrating Combined Therapies for People with Co-occurring Disorders*

- Patient education and cognitive-behavioral therapy (CBT): *Cognitive-Behavioral Therapy for People with Co-occurring Disorders*

- Medication management: *Medication Management for People with Co-occurring Disorders*

- Family education and group therapy: *Family Program*

A Comprehensive Recovery Plan template is provided on the CD-ROM.

The template combines the treatment plans for a patient's substance use and psychiatric disorders on the same form. It uses the *ASAM PPC-3* Dimensions to organize goals and potential objectives and interventions for the substance use disorder and leaves open the option to use the Dimensions to address the psychiatric disorder.

As outlined in *A Leader's Guide to Implementing Integrated Services for People with Co-occurring Disorders,* addiction treatment programs and counselors may not be at a level to provide integrated or enhanced mental health services. The objectives/interventions previously listed may or may not be possible, depending on the capacity of the program. Figure 14 lists treatment objectives by program type (AOS: addiction-only services; DDC: dual diagnosis capable; DDE: dual diagnosis enhanced). Not all programs will be able to meet all of the mental health treatment objectives in-house. Programs and providers should know their scope of practice and its limits.

FIGURE 14

Program Potential to Meet Treatment Objectives for Patients with Co-occurring Disorders

The table below illustrates some potential programmatic objectives possible or not by program (or provider) capacity (**X** indicates possible; **R** indicates referred).

OBJECTIVE	ADDICTION-ONLY SERVICES (AOS)	DUAL DIAGNOSIS CAPABLE (DDC)	DUAL DIAGNOSIS ENHANCED (DDE)
Stabilization	R	R	X
Patient education	X	X	X
Motivation	X	X	X
Coping skills	X	X	X
Illness management and recovery	X	X	X
Family education and support	X	X	X
Symptom management (with medication)	R	X	X

Duplicating this page is illegal. Do not copy this material without written permission from the publisher.

63

On the other hand, once a disorder is present (as discovered in the screening and assessment process), it must be identified on the treatment plan, if only to be monitored and referred. These psychiatric disorders should be considered as complications to treatment, relapse risk factors, and threats to recovery. Programs and providers who must refer need to work in close consultation and collaboration with other providers who are delivering services to address the other objectives.

It is also important to keep in mind patient motivation. Practitioners or programs can record the scores from the Stage of Motivation and Treatment Readiness for Co-occurring Disorders (SOMTR-COD) on the Comprehensive Recovery Plan under substance use Dimension 4 or along one of the objectives for psychiatric disorder, or you could create specific columns or cells for each stage for each problem. Progress notes might also feature a line to record SOMTR-COD scores.

Lastly, as chapter 8 details, working in collaboration with a patient in developing the treatment plan and in jointly monitoring his or her response to treatment is excellent practice. Doing so promotes the therapeutic alliance and likely produces more favorable outcomes. ▼

KEY POINTS ADDRESSED IN CHAPTER 7

1. Problems pertaining to mental health and psychiatric disorders should be reflected on the treatment plan along with substance use problems and disorders.

2. Important objectives for the psychiatric problems include stabilization, patient education, motivation, coping skills, illness management and recovery skills, family education and support, and symptom management.

3. Every treatment plan for every problem should take into account patient motivation.

4. Programs and providers will vary in their capacity to target all of these objectives. They may need to work in collaboration or consultation with other providers.

Shared Decision Making

1. What is shared decision making in health care?

2. How can I use the shared decision-making approach in the initial stages of co-occurring disorders treatment?

The concept of shared decision making is relatively new to health care. It may hold special interest for clinicians treating people with co-occurring disorders.

At this juncture in the screening and assessment process, you have screened for and detected a psychiatric problem within the context of a substance use disorder, performed a thorough assessment, and generated a probable diagnosis. You have also carefully assessed the patient's stage of motivation, not only to address his or her substance use, but also to address the psychiatric disorder. Further, you have inquired about the patient's motivation to address these problems using professional help. The outcome of this process is the generation of a draft of an integrated treatment plan. You will set a course of action that targets both the substance use and psychiatric disorders, and takes into account the patient's stage of motivation for action.

Shared decision making is a type of clinical interaction, philosophical and practical, that might conceivably guide the next step in this process: taking the step from plan into action.

Background to Shared Decision Making

Current health care technology provides multiple intervention options. Consider the problems of obesity, high blood pressure, diabetes, or low back pain. For each of these common conditions, there are multiple lifestyle changes and medications that are helpful. There are also surgical options for obesity and low back pain. In addition, for milder severities of these illnesses, there is the option of "watchful waiting," which simply means observing the problem carefully over time to see if it gets worse, stays the same, or gets better.

For the great majority of conditions and clinical decisions, options involve trade-offs. For obesity, for example, exercise and diet are difficult to maintain

Duplicating this page is illegal. Do not copy this material without written permission from the publisher.

65

and relatively ineffective over the long run, but they involve few risks. Medications are more effective but present a variety of side effects, such as gastrointestinal pain. Surgery is the most effective option but has the most serious side effects, including death during the procedure. Similar trade-offs exist related to available treatments for other conditions. Thus, the typical health care dilemma today is not a lack of reasonable or effective approaches, but rather the choice among several approaches that may have different positive and negative effects.

Given this situation, how should health care choices be made? There are three common approaches.

1. In the traditional "paternalistic" approach, clinicians decide what intervention best fits the patient's condition and advise (order) the patient to adhere to this approach.

2. Alternatively, the "consumerist" approach asks the patient to collect information, make a decision about treatment, and seek the appropriate provider to obtain the treatment.

3. For nearly all common health conditions, most patients prefer a third option of sharing responsibility for health care decisions, which is termed "shared decision making."

Shared Decision Making: Basic Principles

All modern health care is based on the evidence-based medicine model. This model includes three essential components: current scientific information, patient preferences, and clinicians' skills. Shared decision making is the approach for bringing these three components together. The clinical situation involves two experts: a clinician who has experience, skills, and access to the current best evidence on the effectiveness of treatments, and a patient who knows his or her values and preferences regarding goals, risks, participation effort, and interventions. In shared decision making, both parties share their expertise and negotiate a plan that they agree is optimal.

Consider an example from smoking cessation. Several effective interventions exist: physician advice, self-management (sometimes with a computer program), peer support groups, professional counseling, various forms of nicotine replacement, and at least two medications. The patient's treatment provider should know about the success rates and side effects of each of these interventions and should be able to describe these details and provide written information as well as information regarding computer resources. But the clinician would have difficulty knowing which option would be best for a particular patient. The patient might see smoking as a health issue and want to consult a trusted physician, might want to try quitting with a computer-guided self-management approach, or might want to try a medication. The patient's preference might be grounded in very good information about his or her values, habits, strengths, or beliefs. Not paying attention to the patient's preferences could doom his or her recovery because of nonaccess, nonadherence, or low expectations. For example, the patient may dislike taking medications and be unlikely to give a medication a full trial. The clinician may also have an informed opinion regarding peer support group meetings versus group therapy versus individual therapy based on knowing the patient and local resources well.

Rationale and Advantages of Shared Decision Making

Shared decision making has several advantages. It fulfills the first principle of medical ethics that people have a right to control their own bodies. It recognizes individual preferences and includes the patient's self-knowledge in the treatment plan. It activates the patient to take responsibility for the treatment. And it helps to form a collaborative relationship between the provider and the patient.

Some patients may decline to offer strong personal preferences and seek the clinician's best advice. Such a choice can also be part of shared decision making. The patient has expressed a preference for passive decision making. Sometimes the patient may couch this in terms of "Doctor, what would you want your daughter to do if she were in my situation?"

Strategies for Shared Decision Making

Shared decision making entails two steps. First, the two parties (or sometimes more, e.g., when a patient opts to include family) share information, and second, they discuss options and agree on a decision. Both parties need to have accurate, understandable information on scientific issues such as the biological, psychological, and social aspects of addiction; mental health problems; interactions; recovery; and treatment options. There are multiple formats for providing the current science: pamphlets, books, lectures, videos, computerized resources, and expert consultations. Individual clinicians and patients have different learning styles, which means that multiple resources make sense.

Ideally, the latest information should be individualized for the patient. For example, information on medications needs to take into account the patient's liver function status, and information on outpatient versus residential treatment should depend on severity of addiction, history of treatment, and level of community

Duplicating this page is illegal. Do not copy this material without written permission from the publisher.

67

supports. In the future, as individualization of the advantages and risks of various interventions becomes more complicated and more accurate (consider the burgeoning information on cognitive function and genetics), it will be necessary to combine information and present probabilities by computer. For now, clinicians can only put together the best information that is available.

In addition to basic scientific information, the patient needs to add information on his or her goals, values, and preferences. For example, perhaps the patient has tried a particular medication for depression and did not like the side effects. Other medications or even nonmedication options should be considered. Or perhaps another patient desires reduced anxiety in social situations as a top goal, which suggests that cognitive-behavioral therapy and/or medications for this patient's social anxiety disorder need to be part of the initial plan.

Similarly, the clinician adds information based on his or her expertise. This includes explaining the overall assessment and how it fits with the patient's preferences and local resources. For example, perhaps the patient is a woman who has suffered abuse by men and is more comfortable in smaller, women-only situations. The clinician may know of a female cognitive-behavioral therapist or AA group that will be a good match for this patient.

Once the information is clear and opinions are expressed, the parties negotiate a treatment plan. In this process, the clinician recognizes that engagement in treatment, commitment to follow through, and taking responsibility are all critical for the client. Therefore, the plan must be consistent with the patient's preferences. At the same time, the plan must also be consistent with ethical care, current science, and the clinician's expertise. Therefore, the plan must make sense to the clinician. When disagreements appear, the parties need to continue the discussion and resolve conflicts. At times they may need to disagree respectfully and even arrange for a referral to another clinician or program.

Current Guidelines for Shared Decision Making

Shared decision making is a relatively new concept in addiction and mental health treatment. The field may change rapidly as computerized resources, formats for sharing information, and styles of collaboration develop. In the meantime, guidelines are relatively simple.

First, patients and clinicians should have access to information that provides them with the latest evidence about what works and how. For example, what exactly is known about treating post-traumatic stress disorder in persons who have an active addiction? People cannot make optimal decisions about care without such information. What is the difference between medications and cognitive-behavioral therapy for persons with PTSD and substance use disorder? (See *Cognitive-Behavioral Therapy for People with Co-occurring Disorders.*)

Second, patients and clinicians need to have time and a forum to share information on their views and preferences. For example, once informed by accurate information, the patient needs to express any strong preferences about using medications (such as naltrexone or an antidepressant), and the clinician needs to provide relevant information consistent with his or her experience and knowledge (such as research about antidepressant medicines or addiction medicines).

Third, negotiating a plan that accords with all three perspectives (scientific evidence, patient preferences, and clinician expertise) requires time, respect, and competence. This is really the essence of clinical skill, and the success of treatment is often determined by the relationship during this early encounter.

Summary

As the clinician develops the recovery plan with the patient with a co-occurring disorder, it is important to use a shared decision-making approach. In this approach, the clinician reviews the evidence for the treatments proposed, discusses options (including advantages and disadvantages), and collaborates with the patient in selecting the best-fit plan for this particular patient at this particular point in his or her recovery. Moving forward, both parties have to consent to careful monitoring of the effectiveness or outcomes of these decisions in the event that progress is not as positive as envisioned. Chapter 9, on using objective data to monitor change, provides details on how both parties can assess the success of their initial plan. The benefit of working together as collaborators, having a patient who is informed and invested, is likely both improved participation and better outcomes. ▼

KEY POINTS ADDRESSED IN CHAPTER 8	1. Shared decision making is an emerging approach in health care that fosters increased patient collaboration and participation in his or her own treatment.
	2. Shared decision making can be readily used in the treatment and recovery stages of care for patients with co-occurring disorders.

Using Screening Measures to Monitor Symptom Change and Guide Shared Decision Making

Using Screening Measures to Assess Patient Progress

The generic and specific screening measures introduced in chapter 4 can also be used to measure patient progress. The Modified Mini Screen (MMS) is more of a generic tool to diagnose problems, so it is less amenable to being used to watch changes over time. The more-specific Center for Epidemiologic Studies Depression Scale (CES-D Scale), Social Interaction Anxiety Scale (SIAS), and PTSD Checklist (PCL) are designed to measure severity of symptoms and, in fact, have been used in research to measure patient change.

If you use these screening measures for the initial clinical process, you can also use them at intervals throughout treatment. For instance, if you repeat these measures every two weeks in an intensive outpatient program, monthly in a long-term residential program, or every three months in a methadone maintenance program, you will have a measure of patient progress and change.

Keep in mind that in some cases patients may look worse before they get better. This may happen if patients underemphasize mental health problems because of mistrust or fear of not being accepted for treatment or because of the clouding effects of the substances. In thirty days, they may be more trustful, less worried about being dismissed from the program, and less under the influence—so they may score as more severe on the screening measure. But most patients would agree they actually are in a better place than thirty days prior.

In other instances, patients may score more severely because they are actually getting worse. The treatment either is not working or is not the right treatment. The patient may require a more intense level of care or a more specific intervention. Having data to observe this process is not only academically valuable but also clinically valuable.

Duplicating this page is illegal. Do not copy this material without written permission from the publisher.

71

As patients make progress, they feel better. Having data to depict this process is affirming, not only to clinicians but also to patients. People like to see progress. They like to see where they are relative to where they started. Feedback is useful. Students watch their grades from semester to semester, and investors watch interest in their bank accounts or retirement funds change from year to year. Using the screening measures to depict the changes in patient symptoms is a useful and important way to show progress or to track deterioration.

Figure 15 shows charts for three specific screening measures: CES-D Scale, SIAS, and PCL. The vertical axis represents the scores on these measures; the horizontal axis represents the month of assessment. In this sample case, the measure was given at intake and at one month. As you can see, this patient began with low depression and anxiety scores (CES-D Scale, SIAS), and these scores remained the same or improved after one month. On the other hand, this person scored high on the PCL (for post-traumatic stress disorder symptoms) and after one month scored even higher. The PCL graph should alert a clinician, if he or she does not already know, or at least confirm that PTSD symptoms are worsening. Perhaps a special intervention such as cognitive-behavioral therapy is indicated. (See *Cognitive-Behavioral Therapy for People with Co-occurring Disorders.*)

FIGURE 15

Using Specific Screening Measures to Monitor Patient Progress

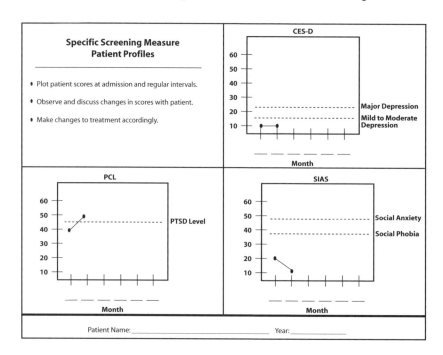

The Summary Scoring Sheet (provided on the CD-ROM) contains blank graphs where you can record the results of a patient's scores from the CES-D Scale, the SIAS, and the PCL. You can plot the scores of the screening measures and include them in the chart of every patient. Further, you can use these graphs to guide your conversations with patients. In this regard, you can use the graph to affirm progress or to express concern or curiosity. You can ask the patient to comment on the graph (either noting increase or decrease in severity) and wonder about what is accounting for it. You can also discuss the potential to change treatment strategies (fewer or more) or approaches if need be. Having data in conversations with patients is extremely useful.

Using Screening Measures to Compare Patients

As a student, you may remember wanting to know how your grade compared with the grades of other students, particularly those you identified with or wished to be like. Later, you learned about percentile rank and discovered that your scores on standardized tests could be compared with the scores of students everywhere who had taken the test. This revelation could have been exciting, validating, or sobering for you. Not wanting to feel alone or different is common to the human experience. Wanting to know how one is doing, relative to others, is interesting and useful information.

As you are gathering screening measure information, you will be in a position to learn the average baseline score among your patient group for the various measures. For instance, you might learn that the average score for new intakes on the PCL is 25. Let's say you have a new patient who scores 65. This patient does not understand why you are recommending a course of treatment that differs from that of other patients. You can show her the PCL graph and indicate not only that her score is above the cutoff for PTSD but also that the average intake score is 25. Thus, having access to the average baseline scores in your program (which a program manager or interested clinician could calculate) would be useful in talking about treatment recommendations.

In addition, if you collect screening measure data over time, you can average the scores of all your patients on the three measures and then plot the lines from admission to one month to two months and so on. You will see what the average change is among your patients, and this trajectory can be used to guide a conversation with an individual patient.

For instance, perhaps the patient who scored 65 agreed to start cognitive-behavioral therapy for her PTSD symptoms. At one month her PCL score is still at 65, indicating no progress. You could talk about whether her PTSD symptoms might take a little longer to improve, discuss her impressions of the matter, and decide if a change in plan is needed or if a steady, patient course is indicated. At two months her PCL score may be down to 30, below the PTSD threshold and now closer to the average of all the other patients treated in the program. This information would not only be affirmative for the clinician and the program, it would also show the patient her progress and help her to understand that she is now at the same level as everyone else (on average).

Accumulating the data to develop the "usual admission score" and "usual change patterns" can be remarkably useful in conversations with patients and in the affirmation of or decision to alter a treatment plan. Using these kinds of data is integral to the shared decision-making approach (see chapter 8). ▼

KEY POINTS ADDRESSED IN CHAPTER 9	1. Specific screening measure data on the CES-D Scale, SIAS, and PCL can be used to chart patient change in a systematic way, and then used to guide conversations with patients about treatment planning.
	2. By collecting specific screening measure data on patients over time, a program or practitioner can average a group of patients' admission scores and plot the usual patterns of change. This information is useful in shared decision-making discussions with patients regarding the need for treatment or changing the existing recovery plan. It can also affirm the treatment plan.

Continuous Quality Improvement and Process Improvement Strategies

Continuous Quality and Process Improvement

Most practitioners and programs would like to deliver the best treatment available to the patients for whom they care. Practitioners get a sense of what is the best treatment available through their education and training, and through professional development opportunities such as workshops and conferences. Programs also learn from experience what works, but they also must follow the rules of regulatory agencies and the financiers of services. Mandates from these authorities play a large role in programmatic changes by shifts in policy. Clinicians and programs also understand that researchers collect and analyze assessment and outcome data, often using time-consuming and expensive assessment and outcome measures. As much as clinicians and agency leaders would like to have this information available to them, most recognize the extraordinary cost in time and expertise to conduct these kinds of inquires. So the typical approach is to measure outcomes with an "n" of one at a time (in other words, according to how each individual patient responds).

As outlined in *A Leader's Guide to Implementing Integrated Services for People with Co-occurring Disorders,* a group of leaders in the treatment of addiction recently assembled a pragmatic list of *process improvement* measures that are relatively easy to implement. This group, known as NIATx (Network for the Improvement of Addiction Treatment), acknowledges these measures to be imperfect and inexact approximations of outcomes, but in the absence of anything else, it considers the list a step in the right direction. By collecting the data suggested by NIATx, providers can learn about the effectiveness of their work without the researcher-level measures that are time consuming and expensive. The data can be used for validation or for change planning.

In the remaining sections of this chapter, we outline several process improvement measures that can be implemented with this guide. NIATx has

Duplicating this page is illegal. Do not copy this material without written permission from the publisher.

75

not considered the role of co-occurring disorders in addiction treatment quality improvement. So what follows is the first-known consideration of the co-occurring disorders issue in the application of process improvement measures.

Identifying Patients with Co-occurring Disorders

The first step in conducting clinician-generated or program process improvement strategies is to identify patients with co-occurring disorders. There are three ways to do this, each with advantages and disadvantages.

1. **Diagnoses:** The screening and assessment measures in this guide will help a clinician or program more accurately identify patients who have psychiatric disorders. These disorders, in conjunction with a substance use disorder, will need to be recorded onto a diagnostic summary sheet or a treatment plan. The aggregate of patients treated (or admitted) should help to reveal those patients with and those without co-occurring psychiatric disorders. The data also will help to determine the relative prevalence of co-occurring disorders in general, and specific diagnostic groupings in particular (e.g., PTSD). The major disadvantage to identifying patients through diagnoses is that frequently not all diagnoses are recorded in clinical records. So if this approach is selected, a program director, supervisor, or individual clinician must ensure that all diagnoses are recorded.

2. **Severity scores:** The MMS and specific screening measures (CES-D Scale, SIAS, and PCL) will help a clinician and/or program to determine the presence of a co-occurring disorder. By recording individual scores and identifying those persons above threshold cutoffs for disorders, a clinician can gather an aggregate of this information over time. This aggregate will provide a list, based on systematic screening data, of the number and percentage of patients above (and below) threshold, and those who are likely positive for co-occurring psychiatric disorders. The disadvantage to this approach is that self-report screening information may be biased at intake or admission for reasons outlined in chapter 3. These biases of under- or overreporting of psychiatric symptoms need to be considered if this approach is taken.

3. **Service utilization:** Most providers will ask about previous (lifetime and especially over the past year) and current treatment. If any given patient reports mental health treatment (medication, therapy, hospitalization), then this patient's status would be listed as positive for a co-occurring disorder.

The advantage of this approach is that the information is easy to obtain; the disadvantage is that it is not likely to identify most patients with co-occurring disorders.

After patients with co-occurring disorders have been identified, the following process improvement examinations are possible.

Access to Care

Research has shown that most persons with co-occurring disorders do not get treatment for either their substance use or psychiatric disorder, but even fewer (about 5 percent) get treatment for both (McGovern, Matzkin, and Giard 2007). Access to care is a major concern in this respect. So as a provider, you want to be able to assess the possible barriers to services for persons with co-occurring disorders. A provider may also want to track changes in access over time.

The simple way to determine access is to look at the number of patients evaluated and admitted over the past month (or three months), using either the diagnoses, severity, or service utilization approach to identify persons with co-occurring psychiatric disorders. A provider can take this number as an absolute number (number of persons with co-occurring disorders admitted) or a percentage of admissions (number of persons with co-occurring disorders admitted divided by number of all admissions, multiplied by 100).

A practitioner or provider can then ask, "Does this percentage reflect expected rates?" and "Am I satisfied with this percentage?" Further, the following question can be addressed: "Do I want to change this rate and measure it over time?"

Retention

Depending on the level of care, retention can mean completing a thirty- or ninety-day stay, or attending three group sessions over the course of two months. For this reason, benchmarks for retention vary by level of care, and they are sometimes set locally for relevance. Outpatient programs often differentiate between engagement and retention.

Engagement pertains to successfully initiating services, such as by attending two sessions in the first month of admission. For intensive outpatient programs, this number may be increased to two sessions for the first week, or making it from week one to week two of the program. For residential programs, the engagement benchmark may be set at completing the first week of care.

Retention is best set by a practitioner or program based on what makes sense

Duplicating this page is illegal. Do not copy this material without written permission from the publisher.

77

clinically and programmatically. What is the sufficient dose? This can only be determined at a local level. A liberal estimate may be 25 percent of all planned services, whereas a more conservative estimate is 75 percent.

Retention rates for persons with co-occurring disorders can be evaluated by using any of the approaches described above. Rates are calculated by dividing the number of patients with co-occurring disorders by the number of all patients. This could include all patients who initiated treatment. Retention rates for persons with co-occurring disorders might be compared with those without co-occurring disorders. Or more specific questions, such as "Do we have better retention rates with women with co-occurring disorders than with men?" can also be addressed.

A practitioner or program can learn about treatment quality by examining retention rates for persons with co-occurring disorders. These findings may either affirm that the program is effective or suggest that new or enhanced services are needed (see the other components of this CDP program: *A Leader's Guide to Implementing Integrated Services, Integrating Combined Therapies, Cognitive-Behavioral Therapy, Medication Management,* and *Family Program*).

Patient Change

By far the most challenging process improvement measure to obtain is patient change. Only if you elect to use the severity approach (repeated administration of screening measures) will this information likely be available to the clinician or program. If patient change is the goal, and if screening measures are used and repeated, some excellent information will be gathered.

For a simple quality improvement study, the differential outcomes for persons with co-occurring disorders and those with simple disorders (a psychiatric disorder without a co-occurring substance use disorder in mental health settings, or a substance use disorder without a co-occurring psychiatric disorder in addiction treatment settings) can be compared. Do certain categories of disorders (e.g., social anxiety disorder) have less change than others (e.g., depression, PTSD)? Questions like this can be more specifically honed to inquire about differential outcomes by gender, culture, or age of patients. The impact of these disorders on abstinence and recovery could also be examined.

This information can be useful to identify program and practitioner strengths as well as the need for new services or practice improvement.

Consumer Satisfaction

A variety of surveys are available to assess consumer satisfaction in treatment services. Two questions are often used to simplify this process:

1. Were you happy with the services you received in this program?

2. Would you recommend this program to a friend or loved one?

How responses differ by client co-occurring disorder status is useful information for quality improvement.

Summary

Providers, both individual practitioners and programs, are advised to collect data and use the information to assess the quality of care and to guide quality improvements. This will ensure that you are doing everything you can to provide the best possible treatment to those who trust in you. ▼

KEY POINTS ADDRESSED IN CHAPTER 10	1. Once patients with co-occurring disorders can be identified, studies of the quality of care can be done. These studies can be used to assess patient access, retention, and outcome.
	2. General and specific screening measures can be used to conduct these studies and ensure that providers are delivering the best possible care to their patients with co-occurring disorders.

Duplicating this page is illegal. Do not copy this material without written permission from the publisher.

79

CHAPTER 11

Conclusions

Patients with co-occurring disorders are common in the general population and even more so in clinical settings. This guide outlined the expected prevalence rates for specific psychiatric disorders among persons with substance use disorders. These are depressive, bipolar, anxiety, PTSD, and personality disorders, all of which are common and have important implications for treatment. Personality disorders, especially antisocial and borderline personality disorders, are common but perhaps less so than conventional clinical wisdom might expect.

Distinguishing psychiatric symptoms from intoxication and withdrawal, the effects of substances over time, their misdiagnosis by previous providers, and patient motivation to withhold or exaggerate symptoms all must be taken into account.

Standardized self-report screening measures and a careful review of the diagnostic criteria for all disorders are critical in the initial clinical process. Personality disorders, though important and not to be neglected, cannot be identified through self-report screening measures but may be accurately diagnosed over a period of time.

Stage of patient motivation and stage of treatment behavior are also two key dimensions at the front end of a therapeutic encounter and undoubtedly continue to be important over time. Systematically assessing these motivations, both for substance use and psychiatric problems, is essential for treatment engagement and planning.

As disorders and patient motivation to address them are determined, the plan for how to achieve goals is developed. This is the treatment or recovery plan. This plan can be an artificial document to appease regulatory agencies, or it can actually be a document of understanding and cooperation between a patient and a professional.

Bringing problems and approaches to dealing with them to a conscious and transparent level of discourse is core to the concept of shared decision making. To the degree to which patients are involved as collaborators or co-investigators in their treatment, participation (i.e., compliance) and outcomes will likely improve.

If systematic information is gathered at treatment entry and over time, these data can be used to help individual patients and providers talk about what to do and how treatment is progressing. If progress is being made, then these data serve to validate, if not encourage, it. If progress is not being made, perhaps treatments need to be adjusted, or the virtue of patience exercised.

Aggregating and combining data over time can be useful in assessing the quality of treatment services. By integrating the data collected about co-occurring substance use and psychiatric disorders with the methods of continuous quality improvement or process improvement studies, programs and providers can inexpensively (relatively) learn about their services. Rational decisions can then be made about continuing the present course or making changes to enhance patient care.

This guide, the first component of the Co-occurring Disorders Program, provides materials and directions to patient care. It is a guide to the initial phases and continued monitoring of treatment. If you use the tools in this guide, you will be able to accurately identify and monitor patients with co-occurring disorders. This is the essential first step: to know about your patients' problems and how to monitor them. Other components of this program will provide specific tools and new skills you can use to treat your patients. Hand in hand, these guides will improve your patient outcomes. ▼

▼

REFERENCES

Alcoholics Anonymous. 4th ed. 2001. New York: Alcoholics Anonymous World Services.

American Psychiatric Association. 2013. *Diagnostic and Statistical Manual of Mental Disorders.* 5th ed. Washington DC: American Psychiatric Association.

American Society of Addiction Medicine. 2013. *ASAM Patient Placement Criteria for the Treatment of Substance-Related Disorders.* 3rd ed. Chevy Chase, MD: ASAM, Inc.

Barlow, D. H. 2002. *Anxiety and Its Disorders.* 2nd ed. New York: Guilford Press.

Blaine, J. D., R. F. Forman, and D. Svikis. 2007. Response: Assessing the Instruments. *Addiction Science and Clinical Practice* 12:31–3.

Cacciola, J. S., A. I. Alterman, J. R. McKay, and M. J. Rutherford. 2001. Psychiatric Comorbidity in Patients with Substance Use Disorders: Do Not Forget Axis II Disorders. *Psychiatric Annals* 31:321–31.

Chinman, M., A. S. Young, T. Schell, et al. 2002. Computer-Assisted Self-Assessment in Persons with Severe Mental Illness. *Journal of Clinical Psychiatry* 65:1343–51.

Clark, H. W., A. K. Power, C. E. Le Fauve, and E. I. Lopez. 2008. Policy and Practice Implications of Epidemiological Surveys on Co-occurring Mental and Substance Use Disorders. *Journal of Substance Abuse Treatment* 34:3–13.

Crouse E., K. M. Drake, and M. P. McGovern. 2007. Co-existing Substance Use and Axis II Personality Disorders. In *Clinical Handbook of Co-existing Mental Health and Drug and Alcohol Problems,* ed. A. Baker and R. Velleman, 309–28. London: Brunner Rouledge.

DiClemente, C. C. 2003. *Addiction and Change: How Addictions Develop and Addicted People Recover.* New York: Guilford Press.

DiClemente, C. C., M. Nidecker, and A. S. Bellack. 2008. Motivation and the Stages of Change Among Individuals with Severe Mental Illness and Substance Abuse Disorders. *Journal of Substance Abuse Treatment* 34:25–35.

Drake, R. E., E. L. O'Neal, and M. A. Wallach. 2008. A Systematic Review of Psychosocial Research on Psychosocial Interventions for People with Co-occurring Severe Mental and Substance Use Disorders. *Journal of Substance Abuse Treatment* 34:123–38.

DuPont, Robert, Paul Brethen, and Richard Newel. 2005. *Drug Testing in Treatment Settings: Guidelines for Effective Use.* Center City, MN: Hazelden.

DuPont, Robert, Thomas Mieczkowski, and Richard Newel. 2005. *Drug Testing in Correctional Settings: Guidelines for Effective Use.* Center City, MN: Hazelden.

Erdman, H. P., M. H. Klein, and J. H. Greist. 1985. Direct Patient Computer Interviewing. *Journal of Consulting and Clinical Psychology* 53:760–73.

Grant, B. F., F. S. Stinson, D. A. Dawson, S. P. Chou, M. C. Dufour, W. Compton, et al. 2004. Prevalence and Co-occurrence of Substance Use Disorders and Independent Mood and Anxiety Disorders: Results from the National Epidemiologic Survey on Alcohol and Related Conditions. *Archives of General Psychiatry* 61 (8): 807–16.

Harris, K. M., and M. J. Edlund. 2005. Use of Mental Health Care and Substance Abuse Treatment among Adults with Co-occurring Disorders. *Psychiatric Services* 56:954–59.

Kessler, R. C., M. B. Stein, and P. Berglund. 1998. Social Phobia Subtypes in the National Comorbidity Survey. *American Journal of Psychiatry* 155 (5): 613–19.

Locke, S. E., H. B. Kowaloff, R. G. Hoff, et al. 1992. Computer-Based Interview for Screening Blood Donors for Risk of HIV Transmission. *Journal of the American Medical Association* 268:1301–5.

Margules, R. D., and J. E. Zweben. 1998. *Treating Patients with Alcohol and Other Drug Problems.* Washington DC: American Psychological Association.

McGovern, M. P., A. I. Alterman, K. M. Drake, and A. P. Dauten. 2008. Co-occurring Post-traumatic Stress and Substance Use Disorders. In *Treating Posttraumatic Stress Disorders in Special Populations,* ed. K. T. Mueser and S. Rosenberg. Washington DC: American Psychological Press.

McGovern, M. P., T. S. Fox, H. Xie, and R. E. Drake. 2004. A Survey of Clinical Practices and Readiness to Adopt Evidence-Based Practices: Dissemination Research in an Addiction Treatment System. *Journal of Substance Abuse Treatment* 26:305–12.

McGovern, M. P., A. L. Matzkin, and J. L. Giard. 2007. Development and Application of an Index to Assess the Dual Diagnosis Capability of Addiction Treatment Services. *Journal of Dual Diagnosis* 3:111–23.

McGovern, M. P., and A. T. McLellan. 2008. The Status of Addiction Treatment Research with Co-occurring Substance Use and Psychiatric Disorders. *Journal of Substance Abuse Treatment* 34 (1): 1–2.

McGovern, M. P., H. Xie, S. R. Segal, L. Siembab, and R. E. Drake. 2006. Addiction Treatment Services and Co-occurring Disorders: Prevalence Estimates, Treatment Practices, and Barriers. *Journal of Substance Abuse Treatment* 31:267–75.

McLellan A. T., D. C. Lewis, C. P. O'Brien, et al. 2000. Drug Dependence: A Chronic Medical Illness: Implications for Treatment, Insurance, and Outcomes Evaluation. *Journal of the American Medical Association* 284:1689–95.

Mee-Lee, David. 2007. *Applying ASAM Placement Criteria.* Center City, MN: Hazelden.

Miller, W. R., and S. Rollnick. 2002. *Motivational Interviewing.* 2nd ed. New York: Guilford Press.

National Improvement of Addiction Treatment. www.niatx.net.

Nunes, E. V., and F. R. Levin. 2004. Treatment of Depression in Patients with Alcohol or Other Drug Dependence. *Journal of the American Medical Association* 291 (15): 1887–96.

Perkinson, R. R., and A. E. Jongsma. 2006. *The Addiction Treatment Planner.* Hoboken, NJ: Wiley.

Prochaska, J. O., J. C. Norcross, and C. C. DiClemente. 1994. *Changing for Good.* New York: William Morrow and Co.

Regier, D. A., M. E. Farmer, D. S. Rae, B. Z. Locke, S. J. Keith, L. L. Judd, and F. K. Goodwin. 1990. Comorbidity of Mental Disorders with Alcohol and Other Drug Abuse: Results from the Epidemiologic Catchment Area (ECA) Study. *Journal of the American Medical Association* 264: 2511–18.

Ross, H. E., F. B. Glaser, and T. Germanson. 1988. The Prevalence of Psychiatric Disorders in Patients with Alcohol and Other Drug Problems. *Archives of General Psychiatry* 45:1023–31.

Samet, S., R. Waxman, M. Hatzenbuehler, and D. S. Hasin. 2007. Assessing Addiction: Concepts and Instruments. *Addiction Science and Clinical Practice* 12:19–31.

Sampl, S., and R. Kadden. 2001, 2002. Motivational Enhancement Therapy and Cognitive Behavioral Therapy for Adolescent Cannabis Users: 5 Sessions, Cannabis Youth Treatment (CYT) Series. Rockville, MD: Center for Substance Abuse Treatment, Substance Abuse and Mental Health Services Administration.

Siegel, K., B. J. Krauss, and D. Karus. 1994. Reporting Recent Sexual Practices: Gay Men's Disclosure of HIV Risk by Questionnaire and Interview. *Archives of Sexual Behavior* 23:217–30.

Substance Abuse and Mental Health Service Administration (SAMHSA). 2002. Report to Congress on the Prevention and Treatment of Co-occurring Substance Abuse Disorders and Mental Disorders. Rockville, MD: SAMHSA.

Turner C. F., L. Ku, S. M. Rogers, et al. 1998. Adolescent Sexual Behavior, Drug Use, and Violence: Increased Reporting with Computer Survey Technology. *Science* 280:867–73.

Waterton, J. J., and J. C. Duffy. 1984. A Comparison of Computer Interviewing Techniques and Traditional Methods in the Collection of Self-Report Alcohol Consumption Data in a Field Survey. *International Statistical Review* 52:173–82.

▼

CONTACT INFORMATION FOR SCREENING AND ASSESSMENT MATERIALS

For more information on the screening and assessment materials mentioned in this guide, please refer to the following list.

Addiction Severity Index (ASI)

The ASI is in the public domain and may be obtained by contracting:
Treatment Research Institute
600 Public Ledger Building
150 South Independence Mall West
Philadelphia, PA 19106-3475
215-399-0980 (phone)
215-399-0987 (fax)
www.tresearch.org/resources/instruments.htm

Alcohol Use Disorder and Associated Disabilities Interview Schedule (AUDADIS)

For information on the AUDADIS, contact:
Bridget F. Grant, Ph.D., Ph.D.
Chief, Biometry Branch, Division of Biometry and Epidemiology
National Institute on Alcohol Abuse and Alcoholism
6000 Executive Boulevard
Rockville, MD 20892-7003
301-443-3306 (phone)

American Society of Addiction Medicine Patient Placement Criteria-3rd Edition (ASAM PPC-3)

For purchasing information, please contact:
ASAM Publications Distribution Center
800-844-8948 (phone)
www.asam.org/PatientPlacementCriteria.html

Beck Anxiety Inventory (BAI)

For purchasing information, please contact:
Harcourt Assessment, Inc.
19500 Bulverde Road
San Antonio, TX 78259
800-211-8378 (phone)
800-232-1223 (fax)
www.harcourtassessment.com

Beck Depression Inventory (BDI)

For purchasing information, please contact:
Harcourt Assessment, Inc.
19500 Bulverde Road
San Antonio, TX 78259
800-211-8378 (phone)
800-232-1223 (fax)
www.harcourtassessment.com

Composite International Diagnostic Interview (CIDI)

The CIDI is in the public domain and can be found on the Internet at www.hcp.med.harvard.edu / wmhcidi / index.php.

Global Appraisal of Individual Needs (GAIN)

For purchasing information, please contact:
Chestnut Health Systems, Lighthouse Institute
720 West Chestnut
Bloomington, IL 61701
309-820-3543 (phone)
www.chestnut.org/LI/gain/index.html

Hamilton Anxiety Scale

The Hamilton Anxiety Scale is in the public domain and can be found in various places on the Internet, such as www.depression-webworld.com / hama_print1.htm.

Hamilton Depression Scale

The Hamilton Depression Scale is in the public domain and can be found in various places on the Internet, such as http://healthnet.umassmed.edu/mhealth/HAMD.pdf.

Mini International Neuropsychiatric Interview (MINI)

For purchasing information, please contact:
Medical Outcome Systems, Inc.
2560 Benjamin Road
Jacksonville, FL 32223
866-463-6464 (phone)
800-886-3585 (fax)
www.medical-outcomes.com

Patient Health Questionnaire 9 (PHQ-9)

The PHQ-9 is in the public domain and can be found on the Internet at www.phqscreeners.com.

Psychiatric Research Interview for Substance and Mental Disorders (PRISM)

The PRISM may be obtained by contacting:
Deborah Hasin, Ph.D., or Sharon Samet, M.S.W.
New York State Psychiatric Institute
Box 123
722 West 168th Street
New York, NY 10032
212-923-8862 (phone)
212-543-5528 (phone)

Stages of Change Readiness and Treatment Eagerness Scale (SOCRATES)

The SOCRATES is in the public domain and may be obtained by contacting its author:
William R. Miller, Ph.D.
Director, Center on Alcoholism, Substance Abuse, and Addictions
University of New Mexico
2350 Alamo SE
Albuquerque, NM 87106
505-768-0100 (phone)
505-768-0113 (fax)
wrmiller@unm.edu (e-mail)

You can access it on the Internet at
www.ncbi.nlm.nih.gov/books/bv.fcgi?rid=hstat5.table.62298

Structured Clinical Interview for DSM-IV (SCID)

For purchasing information, please contact:
American Psychiatric Publishing, Inc.
1000 Wilson Boulevard, Suite 1825
Arlington, VA 22209-3901
703-907-7322 or 800-368-5777 (phone)
703-907-1091 (fax)
www.appi.org/group.cfm?groupid=SCID-I

University of Rhode Island Change Assessment Scale (URICA)

The URICA is in the public domain and can be found on the Internet at
www.uri.edu/research/cprc/measures.htm.

Zung Self-Rating Depression Scale

The Zung Self-Rating Depression Scale is in the public domain and can be found in
various places on the Internet, such as
http://healthnet.umassmed.edu/mhealth/ZungSelfRatedDepressionScale.pdf.